GOD'S
SORELY-TESTED
CHILD

MARION TYMMS

GOD'S
SORELY-TESTED
CHILD

The spiritual life of Annette von Droste-Hülshoff,
with a translation of *Das Geistliche Jahr*

MEMOIRS
Cirencester

Published by Memoirs

MEMOIRS
PUBLISHING

25 Market Place, Cirencester, Gloucestershire, GL7 2NX
info@memoirsbooks.co.uk www.memoirspublishing.com

Printed in England

For Jo

The publication of this book in the summer of 2012 marks
the 25th anniversary of the death of my husband,
Professor Ralph Tymms. I hope it pleases him.

I very much appreciate the careful and sympathetic work of
Chris Newton, Editor at Memoirs Books, in helping me in the
preparation of the text.

MET

CONTENTS

INTRODUCTION

As revolution raged in Europe in the spring of 1848, a woman languished in her room in Meersburg high above Lake Constance. On May 24 that year, after many years of failing health, she died. She was just 50.

The name of Annette von Droste-Hülshoff was little known even during her lifetime, not least because much of her work was published anonymously, or under a disguised name, and circulated, if at all outside her family, in very restricted literary circles. Over 160 years after her death she is recognized as a significant German poet, but her work is still valued only to a limited extent by a German-speaking public and, in England and America, barely at all.

One can find many explanations for her relative obscurity, and certainly one of these must be the linguistic difficulties she presents. Even in German, her syntax, vocabulary and idiom are sometimes problematic, and there have been few concerted attempts to render her work into English. Beneath the challenging language lie other difficulties. The lyric poetry which is arguably her finest achievement lacks the expected quality of melody, although she shows herself extraordinarily alert to sounds and brilliant at evoking them. This is what Clemens Heselhaus, an eminent Droste-Hülshoff scholar, must mean when he speaks of the 'reassuring and lucid power of the word' in her writings (1943, p.34). Her abundant imagery is often extremely taxing. Above all, the content makes demands which, for all her undeniable emotion, reflect a deep intellect verging on the cerebral.

It is hard – and probably not at all desirable – to attempt to separate the work of Annette von Droste-Hülshoff from the woman and the life she led. In her case, we are fortunate in having abundant correspondence both from her and to her to afford a picture of her life and an insight into its complexities. This despite the fact that many of her letters were destroyed after her death by a devoted sister anxious to protect her privacy. What emerges, nevertheless, is the very clear impression of an inner turmoil raging in a woman who contrived – or to some extent was forced by her personal circumstances – to remain untouched by the turmoil in the world outside.

The one exception to the prevailing unfamiliarity with her work is the powerful *Novelle*, *Die Judenbuche* (The Jew's Beech), which has been translated into English many times, lends itself to close study and analysis and serves well as a prescribed text for students of German literature. There would be an argument for taking it as a starting-point for the closer investigation of Droste-Hülshoff, but the present study has a specific aim and the author intends to pursue a different course in the attempt to reveal the nature and impact of Droste-Hülshoff's poetic work, and in particular the place within it of the cycle *Das Geistliche Jahr* ('The Spiritual Year'). A second, and in fact more important, aim is to present the bulk of her religious poems, centrally those of *Das Geistliche Jahr* in English translation.

All translations from German are my own.

CHAPTER ONE

Three poems from the final years: 'Die ächzende Kreatur',
'Gethsemane' and 'Das verlorene Paradies'

Strange though it may seem to begin the examination of a lifetime's
work with its closing phases, there is some justification in the case
of Droste-Hülshoff for looking to her last poems for the key to the
place of her religious poetry within her *œuvre*. The poem 'Die
ächzende Kreatur' is usually believed to be her last 'real' poem,
although during her final months, which were marked by increasing
frailty and declining health, she continued to write far less
substantial 'occasional' poems in response to family events.
However, this startling and lucid statement is effectively viewed
side by side with two other poems, with all three expressing her
religious thought and the preoccupation with spiritual matters
which had dominated a lifetime's creativity. They may be seen as
a crescendo, the culmination of much deliberation and sometimes
anguished thought. It is not too much to see them, taken together,
as setting the seal on the thinking which had spanned the three
decades of her adult life and expressed itself in many contrasting
ways - and sometimes with marked inconsistency - in the cycle of
poems known as *Das Geistliche Jahr*. To begin with the earliest
poems of that cycle and attempt to trace the thinking towards the

1

last entries would seem to be the more logical procedure, yet it gives more weight to the progression of her spiritual life and to her development as a poet to seek the key to both in these three products of her concluding years.

'Die ächzende Kreatur' ('Groaning Creation') arose as the product of communication she had had with her dear friend, the philosopher Professor Christoph Bernhard Schlüter, who was a literary critic and writer himself. It was he who had urged her, possibly in the face of considerable resistance on her part, to persist with the work on *Das Geistliche Jahr*, many years after she had set it aside, and he who saw to it that it was published three years after her death, according to her wish that it appear only posthumously. As with that cycle, however, it is evident that his promptings were taken up in a very different way by his independent-minded friend. When he referred her to the passage in *Romans* 8,22 which speaks of the anguish of all creation, he may have hoped that she would read beyond those lines, to the hopeful expression of the ultimate freedom to be attained through God, the release which will come after agony, the harvest that awaits us.

St Paul's assurance of the love of God, on which this great chapter ends, may have comforted her at other times. However, at this point of her life, with illness and physical weakness reminding her constantly of the approach of death, and on a day damp and chill, her emphasis is on suffering; her own, but also that of all the little creatures on whom she focuses. Her view of the fate of living things leads to this startling statement of original sin and the acceptance of guilt as man's legacy. She apparently sent the poem to Schlüter towards the end of August 1846, and one may well imagine that, not for the first time, he may have been surprised and disconcerted by the direction she had taken in this poem, which she calls 'his' in a letter dated August 1846.

If he had hoped to comfort her, she appears, as so often, to reject comfort in favour of a stark and unembellished view of man's place in the universe. This poet of the 'ever-open wounds' – the phrase which she herself uses in her poem 'Abschied von der Jugend' ('Farewell to Youth', 1841) and which seems appropriate to describe her own deeply vulnerable personality - did not readily adopt an easy path, even though so much of what she says makes it clear that she knows that such a path is there for the choosing. The love of God, like the beauty of nature, underlies her poetry, but something in her complex personality made her question its unambiguous relevance to her.

One is left, then, with the uncomfortable sense of a devout and deeply contemplative woman wrestling with the contradictions which have characterised her writings throughout her life, and not finding the solace one might have wished for her. If one looks at the whole *œuvre*, however, one recognizes that this was probably never going to be possible, and that resolution had always eluded her and would always do so. Schlüter, writing after her death, admitted that she remained a puzzle to him and that that was not least because religion never seemed to bring her freedom or to make her inwardly happy. Though he modified this last phrase with the word 'completely' when he came to reconsider his assessment late in his own life, one would probably have to agree that her religious poems, and particularly *Das Geistliche Jahr*, confirm this impression.

Thus 'Die ächzende Kreatur' may well be her last word on a subject central to Christian thought, the whole question of suffering and guilt, of the place of man in God's creation, and his relationship with all living creatures. The 'Kreatur' of the title – though Droste-Hülshoff herself identified the poem by the first line which evokes so vividly the specific setting of its origin – echoes

Luther's translation, and may be understood both as mankind, Man as the creation of God or, more generally, the entire cosmos. Here English can convey the duality of the German by rendering it either as 'creature' or 'creation', and those who have translated the poem have done both. Here the abstract noun is preferred because it seems to place the whole poem in a broader context, with the solitary figure of the human-being, the speaker who is 'the sorely-tested child of God', at the very heart of it, yet profoundly aware of her place within the whole.

Groaning Creation

On a day when the wind was damp and the rays of the sun
shrouded in grey, God's sorely-tested child was sitting
in a dejected state close to the little garden room. Her heart
was so weary and her breast felt so constricted, her head
so dull and heavy that even around her mind the pressure
of her blood drew veils of mist.

Wind and birds her only companions in this solitude of her own choosing;
a great sigh from nature, and place and time soon vanished.
It seemed to her as though she were sensing the tide of eternity
rushing past her, and yet must hear each drop of blood and every heart-beat.

She sat and thought, and thought and sat. The throaty cricket
was singing in the grass, and from a far-off field came the faint sound
of a scythe. The timid wall-wasp flew anxiously about her face
until she pulled her dress firmly to one side, and the
little creature's nest was uncovered.

And a beetle ran across the stonework, terrified and quickly,
as though it were fleeing, and buried its little head, now deep
in the moss, now in the nooks and crannies. A linnet fluttered past,
on the lookout for food, and, at the sound of the bird's cry,
the insect hid itself with a sharp movement in her sleeve.
Thus it became clear to her that God's curse lay not only upon
humankind but yearns upwards towards the heavens,
groaning for salvation, with heavy, dull agony, in the frightened worm,

the timid deer, in the parched blade of grass in the meadow,
thirsting with its yellowed leaves, in every single creature.

How with the curse which he brought upon himself in paradise,
the Prince of the Earth destroyed his blessed kingdom
and caused his servants to pay the price; how he forced
death and decay, agony and anger through the pure veins,
and how nothing remained for him but guilt,
and the sharp thorn of conscience.

This sleeps with him and wakes with him on every new day,
tears apart his dreams at night and goes on bleeding during the day.
Ah, heavy pain, never softened by the greatest pleasure
nor the boldest pride, when gently, gently, it gnaws and thuds
and bores its way inside him like maggots in wood.

Who is so pure that he is not aware of an image within the depths
of his soul because of which he must beat his breast and feel himself
afraid and wounded? And who so wicked that there is not
one word remaining which he cannot bear to hear but which forces
the blood up into his face with fiery, fearful, profound shame?

And yet there is a burden which no one feels and each one bears,
almost as dark as sin and nurtured at the same breast. He bears it
like the pressure of a breeze, sensed only by the sick body, as unaware
as the cavern is of the cliff, or the fatally-wounded man of the bier.

That is the guilt at the murder of the beauty of the earth
and its gracefulness, the deep and heavy guilt at the oppressive blight
on the animal kingdom, and at the fury which inspires it
and the deceit which tarnishes it, and at the pain which torments
it and the mould which covers it.

If this is indeed the last poem she wrote, its message is a hard one
to bear, for it looks as though, however aware she was of the
wonders of the natural world - and so many of her poems leave no
doubt of this - her ultimate view is a pessimistic one, of a creation
destroyed by the created and condemned by its own fault. She offers
no alleviation here of the guilt which is the lot of Man since the
'Prince of the Earth', Adam himself, erred.

Yet not many months before this she had written a poem which can be dated to the late summer of 1845, not very long, that is, before her illness overtook her and she declined steadily towards her death. One would like to think that this woman, who had wrestled with matters of her faith throughout her life but for whom faith was an abiding strength, though never unquestioned, found solace in the knowledge of redemption which fills the great 'Gethsemane', a poem which speaks, not of condemnation and guilt, but of the ultimate saving power of love. Based on the Gospel accounts of St Mark and St Luke, Droste-Hülshoff's depiction of the Agony in the Garden movingly anticipates the suffering and death of Christ, with details of her own which give the poem a powerful visual quality and also, most importantly, convey her awareness of the Saviour as a human being, with all the fears and doubts of man, yet raised above them by His confidence in God the Father and in the nature of His mission.

Gethsemane

When Christ was lying on His face in the grove of Gethsemane,
with His eyes closed, the air seemed only to be uttering sighs,
and a stream was murmuring its pain, reflecting the pale full moon.
That was the hour when the angel was sent down, weeping,
from the throne of God, in his hand the bitter chalice of suffering.

And in front of the Saviour the Cross rose up, and upon it
He saw His own body hanging, torn in pieces, stretched out.
The sinews on His limbs pressed forward in front of Him like ropes.
He saw the nails projecting, and the crown upon His head,
where a drop of blood fell from every thorn, and there came
the muted sound of thunder rumbling, as though in anger.
He heard the sound of dripping and a soft whimper slid,
tormented, desolate, down the upright wooden Cross.
Then did Christ sigh, and sweat poured forth from all His pores.

And the sky darkened, a dead sun floated in the grey sea,
and the anguish of the Head with the crown of thorns
could hardly now be seen, swaying to and fro in the pangs of death.
At the foot of the Cross lay three figures. He could see them
lying there, grey like clouds of mist. He heard the movement
of their heavy breathing. The folds of their garments fluttered gently.
Ah, what love was ever as fervent as His? He knew them;
He had known them well. The human heart within His breast ablaze,
the perspiration surged more strongly.

The corpse of the sun vanished, leaving behind only black smoke,
and sunk within it the Cross and the soft sound of sighing.
A silence, more terrifying than the raging of the storm,
floated through the starless alleys of the firmament.
Not a breath of life any longer in the wide world,
a crater round about, burnt out and empty, and a hollow voice cried
from above "My God, my God, why hast Thou forsaken me?"
Then the pangs of death overtook the Saviour, and Christ wept,
His spirit broken. Then His perspiration turned to blood,
and trembling came forth from the mouth of the suffering One:
"Lord, if it is possible, let this hour pass me by."

A flash of lightning streaked through the night.
The Cross was floating in the light, radiant with the symbols
of the martyrdom, and He saw millions of hands stretched out,
clinging fearfully to the stem of the Cross. Ah, hands
great and small from the farthest reaches! And round the crown
there hovered millions of souls as yet unborn, like sparks.
A light haze of smoke crept out of the ground, and from the graves
of the departed came the sound of pleading. Then,
with abundant love, Christ raised Himself to His feet and cried:
"Father, Father, not my will but Thine be done!"

The moon floated silently in the blueness. A lily stood
before the Saviour in the dewy grass, and out of the calyx
of the lily stepped the angel and gave Him strength.

Droste-Hülshoff draws on the Gospels for the episode itself and uses
the familiar words of the Son to the Father. She takes from St Luke

the detail of the angel coming, to give strength to Christ (*Luke* 23, 43), but she adds the image of the lily, symbol of purity and holiness. Most powerful of all the visual effects she creates is that of the hands outstretched, the pleading millions of souls departed and yet to come. In this way she places the Crucifixion firmly in the context of the history of mankind, ensuring that the fact that God made Man through Jesus Christ is seen in His relationship with all men, and the message of the Sacrifice is ultimately not of suffering but of Love. This is a wonderfully positive poem which transcends the agonizing sense of guilt of 'Die ächzende Kreatur', with its overwhelming consciousness of the burden laid on all creation since the transgression of Adam. Yet 'Gethsemane' does not flinch from the depiction of physical agony, this time of the Saviour as He prepares Himself for the martyrdom ahead, but looks beyond it to the redemption it represents.

Belonging to the same year as 'Gethsemane' and classed, like it, as a 'Legende', is Droste-Hülshoff's highly individual treatment of the question of human transgression in 'Das verlorene Paradies' ('Paradise Lost'). In it the concentration is on the figure of Eve and her part in the legacy of original sin.

Paradise Lost

When paradise was still opened up to the first sinless pair
the viper knew no poison, the shrub no thorn,
the lion and the tiger knew no rage, and the fluting
of the nightingales still resounded merrily. Then every evening
Eve fell asleep against a rose-bush, and the radiance of her
innocent red cheeks played tenderly around the bright cluster
of the flower, for then the roses were all white and had no thorns.
With the fragrant garland dancing its radiant way above her head and nodding
round her, the first woman reposed deep

in her thoughts which, embryos yet, already bore the divine seal
on their foreheads and already as seeds lovingly touched
the half-closed seraph's wings. She lay there, the bough
pressed to her breast, for no flower had yet been picked,
until softly her eyelids closed, and into her dreams slipped
paradise. Ah, the woman was holy! No one who saw her could have
pondered whether she was beautiful, only that she was pure as dew
and the mirror of God. The rose smiles blissfully too,
but for how long? Beware of the serpent!

The dark lining of the first thunder cloud stood grumbling
on the grey horizon. On the rose bush the first tear fell,
and the moaning of the nightingale wept over there.
Could this be the image of yesterday, this body wrapped
in protective leaves? A wicked woman, her eyes announcing
a forbidden knowledge! How hot and hard seems the cushion
of moss, how filled with darkness the splendour of paradise,
and how strangely do her cheeks burn! Tightly she held
the heavy rose branch, as tightly as the drowning man
clings to the rushes, or an ardent suitor to his love.
Has she fallen asleep? Certainly night has brought rest to her,
and leaden sleep. The shower of rain has not awoken her,
the roll of thunder not alarmed her. Only her hair was fluttering
in the raging wind, and the roses trembled on her breast.
She lay painfully gentle, like a corpse, for the first time in sleep
the image of death. And when the next morning
she opened her eyes and pushed the branches sharply from her breast,
all the radiant light of her cheeks had passed into the flowers
around her, all transformed with passionate longing,
her full lips opening up for a kiss, and Eve was kneeling,
weeping, her cheeks drained of colour and her breast wounded
by the thorns.

'Gethsemane' and 'Das verlorene Paradies' were enclosed in a
letter to the writer and critic Levin Schücking in August 1845, in
response to his request for some poems for publication in his
projected volume of *Das Rheinische Jahrbuch*. In the event, however,
they were not published until after her death, along with a number

of other late poems, and the cycle *Das Geistliche Jahr*. Her letter to Schücking mentions the less than favourable circumstances in which these two 'Legenden' had come into being, often late at night when she was very tired from looking after her ailing uncle and only really, she maintains, because she did not wish to refuse Levin's request. She draws attention to the many alterations she has made, the different versions of a number of lines and even whole passages, and she urges him to choose for himself what, if anything, he wishes to publish. As it happened, she subsequently withdrew her permission for him to use these two poems, unhappy about the anti-Catholic direction the intended publication seemed to be taking. Their eventual appearance, with 'Die ächzende Kreatur', alongside *Das Geistliche Jahr* and a substantial collection of her later poems, must have made a considerable impact on a public apparently so little touched by her death some years earlier.

All three poems are powerful expressions of religious thinking from a woman who struggled all her life to express her spiritual thought in her writing, and they show how original she was in achieving this coalescence of her faith and her thinking. 'Paradise Lost' and 'Gethsemane' are obviously prompted by familiar biblical accounts, and what links them is her retelling of the story of the Fall of Man and of the Agony in the Garden in a way which is at the same time highly selective and extraordinarily creative. She handles the familiar material as though she were relating legends, expanding and adding details all her own, but the word 'legend' which is attached to the two poems is appropriate in another way, too, for the link between them is the traditional relationship between Adam and Eve in the Garden of Eden and their responsibility for sin in the world, and Christ in the Garden of Gethsemane, entrusted with the redemption of mankind. The two episodes are central to Christian thinking, of course, and their juxtaposition needs no explanation. What makes them so striking is her handling of the biblical narrative, the visual effects she creates and the details she adds, and the compassion with which she concentrates on the two figures at the heart of each poem, the one the woman Eve, created by God to be the mother of the human race, and the other the Son of God.

In both poems, a dream dominates, a vision of a future known so well to the reader. The woman sleeps, beautiful and pure, but what lies ahead is not beautiful and not pure. The serpent lurks, and with it come other threats: thunder and darkness, and the first tear. The body of the sleeping woman is like a corpse; only now does the prospect of death hang over her, for knowledge, forbidden to her by God, has transformed her whole being. When she awakes, the emphasis is on her new-found sensuality, the full lips ready to give and to receive a kiss, but the totality of her changed state is expressed in the visual statement of the final lines: the flush on her cheeks which was linked in the early description with beauty and above all with innocence is gone, and the thorns have left their trail of blood on her breast. There is no need to say what this means, for the Bible has spoken of the coming of sin into the world through the action of Eve, and that is the moment of which Droste-Hülshoff is telling, focusing with compassion on an inevitable event which must await reversal in the sacrifice of 'Gethsemane'. There is no suggestion of condemnation of the first woman for her transgression, only the sad awareness of a moment in the history of mankind which made necessary the greater gesture of the Crucifixion.

Thus 'Gethsemane' is by far the more important statement of Droste-Hülshoff's thought, and one would like to think that it was more important to her than that contained in 'Die ächzende

Kreatur', where the sense of the guilt of all living things is not alleviated by the overriding awareness of the love of the Creator. If one takes these three poems together, one gains a key to the religious thinking of this woman, whose whole life was centred on a sometimes highly introspective examination of the place of her faith within it. They may also be seen as a culmination of the work so important to her, the cycle known as *Das Geistliche Jahr*, begun in her youth, continued in her maturity, with the insistence that it be published only after her death. That cycle, too, is characterised by fluctuations of thought, often no doubt dependent on the external circumstances of her personal life, and one looks in vain for a consistent pattern. It represents a substantial body of work, varied in theme and form, and, taken as a whole, reflecting the growth of Droste-Hülshoff as a person and as a poet.

In both respects this growth was truncated by ill health and an early death, but it is still possible to speak of a whole within those limitations. One is aided, in the attempt to understand a very complex literary figure, by a large quantity of correspondence, though there is less than there might have been, thanks to the protective intervention of her sister, who destroyed a great many letters in the days and weeks after her death. What remains, however, gives a vivid picture of Annette von Droste-Hülshoff within the close-knit circle in which she lived, which was itself so closely bound up with the European context of her lifetime. Both emerge in her letters, which reflect both the trivia of her everyday life and the depth and complexity of her mind, albeit with manifold restrictions and inhibitions.

CHAPTER TWO

Annette von Droste-Hülshoff, the woman behind the writings; the poem 'Not'

Annette von Droste-Hülshoff was born on 10 January 1797, the second daughter of an ancient aristocratic family resident near Münster in Westphalia. Her upbringing and home life, like so much that relates to her, were full of contrasts and contradictions. The family was devoutly Catholic and she was brought up to accept traditional religious teachings, while at the same time being aware of her innate leanings towards the supernatural; she recognized that she possessed the gift of second sight and felt herself drawn towards matters expressly forbidden by the Church. While still in her teenage years, she sensed the conflict within her, together with the need to keep secret aspects of herself destined to cause pain to those close to her. This tension within her may well have accounted for the debilitating headaches which plagued her for most of her life, and for the sensation of being on the verge of madness, expressed vividly in her poem for Maundy Thursday, where she seems to be suggesting that God has sent these torments as punishment. Over a year later, she refers in a letter to this poem, recalling a time when her headaches were so severe that she feared for her sanity.

It was not only the consciousness that she possessed acute psychic powers that caused her conflict, however. Her religious beliefs often had to contend with a tension between the pure faith of other members of her family and her own sharp intellect, which was well suited to scientific analysis, particularly in the area she favoured, of the natural world, and this in an age when orthodox religious values were being challenged in Europe. Although there is no actual evidence that she participated in these wider discussions, it is almost inconceivable that a woman of her connections and her enquiring mind would not have been aware of them.

Always introspective, she was able to sum up this conflict in the succinct statement in her poem for the Third Sunday after Easter in *Das Geistliche Jahr*, 'mein Wissen mußte meinen Glauben töten' ('My knowledge had to kill my faith'), a statement which provides an important key to her religious poems, but also gives an insight into her understanding of her own nature, and doubtless to much of the turmoil which seems to have accompanied her throughout her life, and which, for all the awareness of the love of God in 'Gethsemane', was probably never resolved.

From the earliest accounts of her person and her behaviour, Annette von Droste-Hülshoff appears to have aroused contradictory impressions. As a young girl, she was striking to look at, without being conventionally good-looking or even attractive. An awkward reserve and a marked precocity, though undoubtedly related, made for an uncomfortable companion in the frequent family gatherings, which often included distinguished outsiders. An early observer, Friedrich Beneke, a merchant from Hamburg who was visiting the Droste-Hülshoff family, writes at length in his diary of what was evidently an impressive first meeting with her at eighteen. He admits that he came to that meeting with certain prejudices, having been warned by her uncle Werner that she was a formidable young woman, gifted and clever, but almost masculine in her demeanour and inclined to be unattractively forward in manner and opinions. She was capable of being amusing but generally possessed 'more intellect than charm'.

His first sight of her, with her slight figure and the piercing blue eyes so often referred to, clearly took him by surprise, as must her challenge to him to tell her what he thought of her, and why he seemed so antagonistic. It was to this man that the young Annette confided her anxiety about her psychic gifts, filling him, he wrote, with horror at some of the episodes she related from her own experience. The ambivalence of this encounter is apparent in both of them, and Beneke recalls both the lowering effect it had on his own mood and the memory of her subsequent charming behaviour as she entertained the assembled company with her playing and singing.

His passing acquaintance with the young woman he calls the *Zauberjungfrau* ('magic maiden') has left him with a confusion of thoughts, and we must be grateful for the chance find of this entry in his diary for a vivid insight into the perplexing nature of a woman who puzzles on many levels. (See Gödden, pp.114-5)

That Annette was herself aware of her contradictory nature and may even have known that it accounted for some of the deepest and most distressing experiences of her life, emerges too from remarks within her poetry, and from the way she depicts some of the characters in her prose writings and her largely unsuccessful attempts at drama. A comment in a poem as late as 1842/43 addressed to her close friend Levin Schücking sums up her awareness that she can be disconcerting in her response to people and suggests that she knows she can offend or hurt even those she loves: "That there is much in me which is abrupt and blunt, ah!

who could know that as well as I do? Yet, for the salvation of my soul, a second, gentler conscience was bestowed upon me, and this softens the arrogance which controls me like a Titan, and as remorse does battle, it often struggles with this demon." ('An denselben', which begins '*Daß manches schroff in mir und steil....*')

Her letters, too, make it clear that she knows she can over-react, and certainly she often engaged in fierce defence of her writings with those who, like Levin Schücking, respected her work and whose opinions she actually respected, too. Again, however, there was a tension between her intellectual responses and her emotional ones, and, although she was capable of lasting friendships and deep love, she was also able to endanger relationships through her own inner turmoil. For many people who seek to penetrate this very complex personality, it was her early experience of love which cast its shadow over her being and her creative work and meant that, for all the brilliance of some of her finest achievements, the signal absence of a lasting serenity remains an overriding feature.

One can only speculate as to whether both her personal life and her creative progress would have been different if she had not suffered the terrible emotional upheaval when, as a young woman in her early twenties, she felt herself drawn in differing ways to two very different young men, Heinrich Straube and August von Arnswaldt. What exactly happened, and how she managed to alienate both of them, is unclear, and only a lengthy letter to Anna von Haxthausen (from the end of 1821) provides an insight into the devastating effect on her of an experience which, she felt, burdened her with guilt and the opprobrium of those in her circle who knew something of the circumstances and their outcome, but, she believed, not the whole story. It is apparent that, in her youthful inexperience and lack of judgment in terms of human relationships, she mishandled the situation, but the searing pain at the time, and its lasting effect on her, were probably the consequence of her highly developed analytical mind and an inherent tendency to self-accusation.

Such details as this long letter contains suggest that she was genuinely confused by the conflicting feelings she had for the two young men. Finding it impossible to distinguish feelings of friendship from a deeper emotion, she was extraordinarily unguarded in the way she expressed herself to Arnswaldt when he spoke to her, as he seems to have believed, in order to establish her inclination or otherwise towards his friend Straube, presumably not expecting that this would lead to her disclosing her feelings both for Straube and Arnswaldt. There appears to have been no malicious intention on the part of either young man, but both were naturally also confused and wounded by what she had said and clearly decided that the wisest course would be to put an end to the puzzling triangle of relationships. Annette was left devastated and no doubt also feeling humiliated by her mishandling of the whole episode, which appears to have left her with a lasting cautiousness and even to have led, at a later stage, to her admission to her sister Jenny, to whose family she remained devoted throughout her life, that marriage was not for her: she had, she said, 'too little health and too much independence of mind'.

Whether her precise diagnosis was right it is hard to say. Certainly this was a woman who was attractive to men and capable of maintaining enduring friendships, but whose emotional life was probably, in the end, secondary to her intellectual life.

Despite the impact of this early experience on her, one cannot avoid the impression that the effect was ultimately more positive than negative in terms of her literary development, and that the poems which eventually followed were given their remarkable character by what she had endured, or believed she had endured. A more obviously 'satisfactory' outcome might have spelled the end of an extraordinary career not yet begun. The obsession with guilt, however out of proportion to the events, and the ambiguous self-analysis and brooding which one associates with Droste-Hülshoff would probably not have found expression in the contented domestic existence which was denied to her.

Although the turmoil into which this experience, often described as the *Jugendkatastrophe*, cast her was very real, it is difficult to determine whether her mishandling of her emotional life during the months of 1819 and 1820 led to a lifetime of acute introspection and the obsession with her feelings of guilt, or whether these aspects of her character, already evident in her even at this very early age, caused her to behave in a way which was doomed to destroy her own happiness and that of those who cared for her. A remarkable poem associated with that period - whether it was composed before or after the collapse of her friendships with both Straube and Arnswaldt is unclear - bears the title 'Not' (1820). The word itself goes to the heart of the content, yet it is extraordinarily difficult to translate. No single English word - 'need', 'anguish', 'grief', 'suffering'- quite conveys the meaning. It is all these things, but more besides, and the rendering by Ursula Prideaux in the book by Margaret Mare - 'dire distress'- is too descriptive to suggest the impact of the German word, which is shocking in its force and brevity. What is not difficult to assess is the agonizing sense of isolation of which the poem speaks. Even the word 'agony', eventually chosen here, is not quite right either.

Agony

Why do you talk so much of fear and agony in your blameless doings?
You pious people, strike care down dead, (for) it certainly
does not wish to remain with you.

Yet while the agony, over which compassion weeps,
is only like the drop on the hand of the drinker, the dark flood,
which no one notices, stands hidden right up to the very edge of the soul.

You pious people profess that you know care,
and yet you have never seen guilt, but they, those others,
can already put a name to life and its terrifying heights.

A noise as though of song and praise rises up,
and the rays of light play around the flowers. The people dwell silently
in the valley, and up above the dark vultures are nesting.

The stark hopelessness anticipates the tone of later poems, and one senses already the hand that was to write 'Die ächzende Kreatur', but there is a difference. This is not a general statement of the guilt of mankind, the burden that rests on all creation, but a more personal lament by one who feels herself segregated from ordinary people who go about their daily lives untouched by the agonising weight of fear and care. Clearly guilt is there, not experienced by these blameless people, but it is an individual guilt, though undefined.

The long letter to Anna von Haxthausen in which Annette speaks so fully of her experiences of the summer of 1820 makes it clear that she accepted the responsibility for the events which had left her so desolate, and guilt in many forms was to become a pervading theme of many of her poems from this time on. It is no accident that these months saw the beginning of the project which was to occupy her, though with a lengthy interval, for almost the remainder of her life, and it is apt that this poem, slight in form but forceful in its content and tone, belongs chronologically with the early poems of *Das Geistliche Jahr*. It is actually written in some manuscripts alongside them and sometimes included as part of the cycle, thus accounting for the fact that some would argue that this comprises 73 poems, rather than the usually agreed 72.Perhaps one may see it as a kind of justification for the cycle, and even go so far as to see the cycle as some kind of attempt at expiation.

CHAPTER THREE

Early religious poems

It did not, however, begin like that. A letter of 8 February 1819 to her valued friend Professor Anton Mathias Sprickmann, who had done much to introduce her to the world of literature, refers to some religious poems written explicitly for her grandmother, the pious second wife of her mother's father, Werner von Haxthausen, on whose estate and among whose large family Annette spent a great deal of time. These eight poems did not find their way into the cycle, and indeed they do not belong within it, but in some ways they anticipate it in their themes and, occasionally, in their manner. Even at this early stage, and in poems which are in many respects conventional expressions of her religious belief and her love of natural phenomena, there are hints of the anguished self-examination and awareness of guilt which were to become recurrent features of her poetic work.

The titles indicate the nature of these poems, which she apparently did present to her grandmother in an album sadly no longer extant. The first, identified only by its opening line, '*Das Morgenrot schwimmt still entlang....*' ('Dawn silently floats along...') is a joyful welcome to the day, yet even here there is the awareness of the human being, alone and foolish, and needing to be exhorted to the praise of God the Creator. The same relationship between the Creator and the individual is present in the next poem of this group, 'Morgenlied' ('Morning Song'), which begins with another joyful evocation of the transforming power of nature in the early light of day. Yet swiftly the focus moves to the individual observer of this splendour, the 'faithless child' for whom this day has been created, faithless because each day reveals the sinfulness of that child. The third strophe is a plea for God's help:

> Be with me, Lord, Thou who hast granted me a new day.
> The spirit is alert, the flesh is weak, and my efforts bear no fruit,
> and yet Thy hand is firm and strong, if only I will grasp it. Ah,
> Thou hast never abandoned the one who does not himself
> abandon Thee.

In some ways a simple expression of conventional faith and confidence in the omnipotence of God and His unfailing support, the second half of this poem betrays the guilt which hangs over so much of Droste-Hülshoff's lyric, together with the awareness of suffering. This suffering, the 'small hurts' to which she refers ('*kleine Kränkungen*' in line 33), is juxtaposed to thoughts of the Cross, and of the Grace which is assured through the gift of God's own suffering. This is not remarkable thinking for a person of her background, yet it does foreshadow the anguished tussle with faith that will inform so much of her writing as she develops as a poet, and, probably more importantly, faces up to the nature of human existence and her role within it. Thus the poem concludes:

> Lord, release me from false modesty, from arrogance
> and from impatience, and let all my thoughts be turned towards
> Thy Cross and my guilt. Whosoever this day scorns and hurts me,
> let me forgive him willingly and faithfully, and let him repent
> his misdeed before Thee before night falls.

I will go about my duties in praise of Thee and at Thy behest.
No matter how the world may order them about me, I wish to see
only Thy will. Whatever I may do in my home and for my children,
that all rests in Thy wise hands. Whatever commences with praise
of Thee must end to Thy glory.

The companion-piece of this poem is 'Abendlied' ('Evening Song') and it produces, likewise, few surprises, linking as it does the time of day with her total surrender to the will of God, and speaking of her love for Him. The form is simple, and the language without the complexity and particularly the imagery which so characterise her later writings:

I know Thou art not angry if I close my eyes, and in my sleep
Thou wilt restore to me the strength to perform my tasks.
Banish the night of bad dreams from those who honour Thee:
they cannot fight against them, for they are locked in sleep.

I trust Thy hand, for all Thy goodness and Thy love are known to me,
and I know that it will protect me, and that a sure treasure will turn evil
away from me. 'Into Thy hands, O Lord!' Let that be my final word.

The precise chronology of the writing of these eight poems is impossible to establish, but it is apparent that they all belong to the months leading up to Christmas 1819 and that she was sufficiently confident of their suitability to copy them into the album which she presented to her grandmother on that occasion, in the very personal volume, regrettably no longer extant, known as the 'Weweralbum'. The album apparently contained many blank pages, a sign that her plan for a much longer cycle was already there. This, it would appear, was an early demonstration to her closest circle of her preoccupation with religious poems, but to herself it must also have shown how far she was capable of deviating from the norm of her times, and that some of her ideas were dangerously 'modern'. Although the three poems already treated are fairly conventional expressions of faith and the relationship between God and His creation, the two which are usually placed next, and may well have followed in her own conception, reflect different thinking, more personal and self-examining. Most importantly they venture into the themes of guilt and remorse, and above all of suffering, which will become the hallmark of Droste-Hülshoff's poetic work.

Even the titles – 'Für die armen Seelen' ('For the poor souls') and 'Beim Erwachen in der Nacht' ('On Waking in the Night') – reflect this transition in thinking, while at the same time the poems are sufficiently conventional to pass the test she appears to have set for presentation to her devout grandmother. In 'Für die armen Seelen' the conventional thinking, particularly the sense of the close relationship with God and the awareness of the physical suffering of Christ, shows the still very young Droste-Hülshoff under the influence of the poets of the 17th Century. Poets such as Paul Gerhardt and Friedrich von Spee will surely have figured in her early reading matter, although, as far as we know, it was considerably later that she became acquainted with the mystical writings of Angelus Silesius, thanks to the recommendation of her friend, the theologian Christoph Bernhard Schlüter. There is nothing in the language and imagery of this early poem to suggest the originality of the later Droste-Hülshoff, even though it anticipates some of the thought which imbues the cycle which was about to come into being. Thus she speaks of the departed humans, the 'poor souls' of the title, and commends them to God the Father:

My Father, look upon Thy most wretched children
And think of them in their immense suffering;
They were, as we are, sinners,
And death closed the gate of mercy to them.

And even if they left Thy path
And did not look upon Thy hand,
No life, alas, can contain their longing,
And no human sound can utter their remorse.

Oh, Jesus, think of Thy bitter agony,
And of the harsh death upon the Cross!
Alas, Thou hast borne them all within Thy heart,
And for them all the spotless Lamb has died.

Open up Thy five holy wounds
And on five shining, blood-red streams
Send forth Thy Cross to cure them:
A safe ship in their great anguish!

The poem concludes with a statement of her surrender to the will of God and her acceptance of suffering, expressed here in her readiness to share in the suffering of Christ through the grasping of His chalice. The repeated phrase *'ich bin bereit'* ('I am ready') anticipates the acquiescence which runs through so much of *Das Geistliche Jahr*, and it is that sentiment, too, which dominates in the more complicated poem which follows ('Beim Erwachen in der Nacht': 'On Waking at Night'), when thoughts of the nature of night itself lead her to an examination of her relationship with God, and, more specifically in the final strophe, to the comforting assurance of the protection of Jesus.

These are not remarkable poems, but they reveal a devout young woman struggling, as she will again and again, to define her understanding of God and of her own faith. The titles of the remaining three poems in this group, three abstract nouns - 'Faith', 'Hope', 'Love' - sum up the essence of that faith in familiar terms, but their content is less conventional, challenging as it does the nature of human existence with its limitations and disappointments. Thus 'Glaube' ends:

> I know, my Lord, that on this earth
> There is much for me that is hard and bitter,
> And that in its travail my heart
> Often fails to see Thy goodness.
> Yet still I believe that night will in due course
> Dawn before Thy radiance,
> And my lips pronounce in praise:
> The Lord has made all well.
>
> Yes: He has ordained all things well,
> And His word is faithful and true,
> Thus, do not despair, my heart,
> But trust in your sure treasure.
> Yes, my God, I will believe only in Thee,
> And not in human beings.
> And that nothing can rob me of Thy faithfulness,
> In that my heart may truly rejoice.

There are few indications here of the questions which would beset her so consistently later. Her beloved step-grandmother was probably well pleased to see the young girl adhering to the teachings of her roots and echoing the traditional expression of much earlier generations. It is only perhaps with hindsight that one can detect what lies beneath the confidence of the opening of 'Hoffnung', with its ring of language and thought familiar from many decades earlier:

Let life falter,
Let it vanish altogether,
I shall nevertheless gaze, earnest and bold,
Across its silent barriers.
And if mere thinking does not
Find directions in the dark land,
Then Hope knows the pathways
And holds up a sure light.

When all things abandon me,
My hope will remain,
Will embrace me with its saving power,
When anguish and sin oppress me.
And even if death and tribulation rage,
And the evil one gains power,
Lord, on Thy Goodness
I shall build my city.

Indeed, it would not have required much discernment for her selected group of readers to see beyond the familiar phrases of the strophe with which this poem concludes:

And when my end has come
And my pale lips can barely utter
Thy name any more,
Ah, then shall I see with joy
How my hope survives,
For a pious trust
Will not fail.

They would perhaps wonder at, and even worry about, the precocity of the young relative in their midst. However, it would seem that those who had access to the poems she chose to disclose at this stage did not see much more than the signs of talent in one so young. Droste-Hülshoff herself was already deeply aware of the doubts within her, and clearly aware that she had to keep them to herself.

CHAPTER FOUR

Das Geistliche Jahr
The Spiritual Year

Thus she arrived at her decision to write a series of religious poems, though early on in the process she realized, as a letter to her mother makes very clear, that they were totally unsuited for their original purpose and that her beloved, pious step-grandmother was a most unfitting recipient. Her grandfather's second wife, with whom she spent many contented times and in whose large family she was very much at home, was a deeply religious woman, to whom the anguish and doubt already manifesting themselves in her poems would be totally alien and almost certainly very troubling.

She explains in this letter that she has not been able to suppress her tormented thoughts, and commends the first half of what would eventually be called *Das Geistliche Jahr* to her own mother, believing that, since this is the product of her child, she is the rightful owner (Letter dated 9 October 1820). The response, or rather the non-response, of Therese von Droste-Hülshoff was not encouraging and even perhaps deeply shocking to her. This emerges from a letter shortly after, in which she tells Anna, one of her young aunts and a frequent correspondent, that her mother read the poems and the accompanying letter of dedication attentively and then, without a word, placed them in a drawer. If no comment passed between mother and daughter, the message was clear. Annette subsequently retrieved the manuscript, accepting that she had misfired completely with the gesture and reproaching herself with the insensitivity of inflicting her own pain on her nearest and dearest (Letter to Anna von Haxthausen at the turn of 1820/21). She had no right, she writes, to distress others in the attempt to spare herself.

When she now abandoned work on the cycle - whether in her own mind this was to be permanent or not is unclear - she doubtless did so because of the turbulence of her own thoughts at this point as well as the response of her mother.. A further reason was almost certainly that she was aware of other paths which lay before her in her development as a poet. Certainly the fifteen years or so before she resumed work on *Das Geistliche Jahr*, tentatively at first and with the encouragement of Professor Schlüter, were very productive ones for her, but the hesitation with which she approached the task of actually completing the cycle suggests that she was held back by issues relating more to her spiritual thinking than to her reputation as a poet.

Likewise, her insistence that the completed cycle, on which she eventually worked again with great commitment in 1839, should not be published during her lifetime, betrays a lasting uncertainty about the impact of her sometimes startling religious views upon those close to her. She can hardly have failed to know that Professor Schlüter, her dear friend and trusted confidant, was troubled, not to say shocked at times, by her uncomfortable thoughts. Yet it was he who, more than anyone, urged her to continue with this work, arguably her most significant achievement, and it was to him that she entrusted the task of ensuring its eventual publication.

In a study intended primarily for English-speaking readers, it would be remiss not to mention at this point, if only in passing, the coincidence that in the early decades of the 19th Century John Keble was working on his cycle of poems *The Christian Year*. It was published, at first anonymously, in 1827 and warmly acclaimed. Since there is no evidence that Annette von Droste-Hülshoff was familiar with this work, the possibility of direct influence is unlikely. Though the idea of a structure based on the sequence of readings in Church throughout the year may have been talked about in the kind of circles she frequented, Droste-Hülshoff's concept is much more personal and her thinking much less orthodox. Notwithstanding Keble's appointment to the Chair of Poetry at Oxford, and the esteem in which he was held as a theologian and a poet, his place in English literature is a far lesser one than hers in German literature. Her great cycle is justly, though admittedly not universally, acclaimed for its profound and complex thinking, and the struggle of an often tortured individual. It represents, within her *œuvre*, a very significant achievement, the more remarkable for the fact that it spans a lifetime. Keble's work, though by no means to be dismissed, is remarkable for the place it occupies in an era of change and re-assessment within the Church, particularly in England. The chronological coincidence of the two works is probably no more than that, and their respective impact is quite different. Whereas Keble's work has distinct didactic elements, as befits his central role as a clergyman and a leader of thinking within the Church in this period of change, Droste-Hülshoff's cycle reflects her own evolving thoughts on God and her relationship with God and His creation.

The whole cycle and many poems within it are characterised by a questioning tone, exposing her doubts and self-accusation; this is not a woman who sets out to instruct others, so profound is her awareness of her own fragility and the uncertainty which torments her. If at times a poem arrives at what appears to be a resolution of her inner conflicts, what emerges is closer to a gentle indication of a way she has found, at least for the time being, of handling her own confused and troubling thoughts. Emil Staiger, a distinguished Germanist of his generation and one of her most perceptive critics, puts his finger on the essential ambivalence of the cycle, when he says that 'in almost all the poems, for and against are held in a fine balance' (p. 39). She does not address herself to a group of people with the intention of urging them in a particular direction, nor does she suggest that she has herself found a single way. What she does do, in the letter to her mother which stands as a dedication to *Das Geistliche Jahr*, is speak of those whose love is greater than their faith, those – and she says that there are probably many such people, though they do not reveal themselves – who in a single hour ask more questions than seven wise men can answer in seven years. With these people she undoubtedly allies herself, but they are not individuals known to her, unlike her beloved step-grandmother with her simple, unquestioning faith, or her friend Christoph Schlüter, with whom for most of her adult life she shared conversations and correspondence but for whom, by his own admission, she remained an enigma.

She must have known that her mother would be deeply affected by the poems she sent her in 1820, the first half of a cycle which would grow and deepen before it saw its first, posthumous, publication. Even so, her mother's absolute silence may still have surprised her. The accompanying letter ends with her admission that she has not held back in her revelation of her innermost thoughts, though she clearly knows that these may be very painful to those who read them - 'for I have spared no thought, not even the most secret'- an idea which she extended in a letter a few weeks later, in which she links the poems to her devastating experience at the end of her relationship with Wilhelm Straube and August von Arnswaldt. She writes to her aunt, Anna von Haxthausen, that they reflect her whole state of mind at that time, and that her 'shattered, guilt-laden being is laid bare in them'. This sentiment is probably closer to the truth than the somewhat flippant last sentence to her mother, which tells her that, if she has been misguided in her intention, she will justify it by referring to 'the old proverb' which speaks of a rascal 'who offers more than he possesses'. If this was an attempt to deflect the impending maternal disapproval and grief, it almost certainly also failed.

From the letters which survive from the time when Droste-Hülshoff was embarking on her project, and particularly the dedication to her mother, which traditionally presages the 'completed' cycle, it emerges how intensely personal was the impulse to write these poems, at the time without any real sense that they were to constitute a coherent cycle. It is more than likely that she would not herself have included the dedicatory letter had she been responsible for the publication that she had expressly forbidden until after her death. In fact the letter was not included when the cycle first appeared in print, in 1851, almost certainly reflecting her own view that this was not for public consumption. In this respect, as in most others, her devoted friends, Christoph Bernhard Schlüter, to whom she had entrusted the manuscript and who was in regular correspondence with her until shortly before her death, and Wilhelm Junkmann, who collaborated with the almost blind Schlüter in ensuring that the work appeared in print, probably acquiesced in her wish to maintain this privacy.

However, the dedication provides significant clues to the genesis and very existence of the cycle, and read after her death and so many years after it was written, it can be seen as an integral part of the whole, a poignant expression from a young woman barely embarked on her poetic vocation. It supports the position of *Das Geistliche Jahr* within her development both as a poet and as a person, and contributes to the complex picture that we have of a development cut short by ill-health, death, and even by the doubts expressed within the cycle. It is testimony to the devotion of her friends, and to their understanding of her (which may well have exceeded her own), that they saw the absolute need to publish this work, arguably the single most complete expression of her greatness, despite the reservations of some of her commentators (see below, p.114-117) and to do so as soon as possible after her death, when there was in any case some pressure from members of her family to accentuate the religious aspects of her work.

For Droste-Hülshoff herself, the cycle to which she undoubtedly attached great significance from the time of its inception was not, and perhaps never could be, complete. However, once she had succumbed to the urging of Schlüter, she worked on it at times with great commitment and spoke of it as finished in January 1840 (in a letter to Henriette von Haxthausen and evidently to Schlüter himself, since an entry in his diary includes this information). She was writing the very next year to Schlüter of her intention of returning to it and working further on its details (the word she actually uses is 'feilen', literally 'to file', 'to smooth' rough edges). We know from existing manuscripts how attentive she was to the details of her work and how much she changed them, but in the event she did not get round to it in the case of this cherished project. She must have been distracted by her frenzied productivity in Meersburg during the winter of 1841 to 1842, and the pressure of publishing the second edition of her poetic works in 1844, not to mention the emotional impact of her friendship with Levin Schücking and the turmoil of their parting, and her own increasingly fragile physical state. Yet, for all this, she was still speaking to Schlüter as late as September 1844 of her hope that she could write up the definitive version for him, though always with the injunction that he should keep this until after her death.

A telling final piece in this strange and poignant story is that, in the event, the only poem which received the hoped-for treatment is that for the Twenty-Fourth Sunday after Whitsun, which she entered in the family album of her nephew Heinrich von Droste-Hülshoff, her brother's son. The deeply personal tone of the messages within this poem makes it an appropriate choice and closes the circle which had begun when, as a girl still in her teens, she was inspired to write for her step-grandmother, and, failing this, for her own mother.

Broadly speaking, her original concept for *Das Geistliche Jahr* was achieved. In the simplest terms, she had set out to write a poem for every Sunday of the year and every feast day in the Church calendar, taking her texts, it seems, not from the Catholic missal but from the almanac used in the Münster diocese (See Cornelius Schröder pp. 257-265). By the time she set the work aside in late 1820, she had written twenty-five poems, beginning with the one for New Year's Day and ending with Easter Monday. She appears to have been reasonably satisfied with them, since they remained in the state she had achieved at this point, after minimal revision and copying up. When she returned to the project in 1839, she seems to have realized how much remained to be done, and the forty-seven poems she wrote to complete the cycle were accomplished sometimes at considerable speed, often with many alterations and alternative readings, a process characteristic of her method of working at this late stage of her career. If, as we know, she was not completely satisfied when she relinquished her work on this cherished project, this may be attributed both to the artistic perfectionism of the mature poet, but perhaps even more to the fact that it is the expression of a spiritual journey never to be completed in life.

By now Droste-Hülshoff was an accomplished writer, whose range had included powerful epic poems, attempts at drama and the novel, but, most of all, mature lyric poetry with a sure touch and a distinctive stamp. Above all, she had revealed the capacity to evoke natural settings in all their detail and with an acute sense of atmosphere. The woman behind these poems was evident, but her reputation was consolidated by her last poems, written during the brief and overwhelming relationship with Levin Schücking, and in the very few years after their final meeting, when, as she saw it, his inspiration remained with her. *Das Geistliche Jahr* belongs with these poems and completes the picture of an intriguing and many-faceted talent. That said, it must be admitted that evaluations of the cycle differ widely, often according to the fluctuations in literary criticism but also, inevitably, because this cycle has been viewed very differently by those who see it as the expression of a spiritual journey and those who evaluate it simply as a work of literature. (See below, pp 113-117).

We come now to the poems themselves, presented here in English translation. This enterprise requires some explanation, though justification is surely not needed. The intention is to provide a rendering as close as possible to the original, in order to convey the progression, if one can even call it that, of Droste-

Hülshoff's thought, and the essence of each poem. The introductions to the individual poems are relatively slight, not meant to be commentaries but to direct the reader towards some of the central features in each case, an intention which inevitably gives rise to considerable differences in content and emphasis. Where appropriate, reference is made to the published work of critics who have concerned themselves with individual poems, though no claim is made to comprehensive treatment of Droste-Hülshoff scholarship.

No attempt is made to emulate the poetry of the cycle in respect of rhyme or metre, but, as far as possible, features such as imagery and poetic language are retained. Much of this is lyric poetry of a very special kind, lacking obvious melody, but, as with much of her poetry, especially of her maturity, possessing a strong quality of sound, not always very easy to convey in translation.

The seventy-two poems of the cycle show considerable variety in tone and tempo, and to convey this variety a somewhat unusual procedure has been chosen, reflecting the shape of the poems on the page. Although the poems are rendered into English prose, it is hoped that at least something of the impact of the original poetry remains.

CHAPTER FIVE

Das Geistliche Jahr
1820 poems

The cycle begins with a dramatic farewell to the old year and an exuberant greeting to the new one. This is one of the relatively few occasions when Droste-Hülshoff does not attach a biblical reference to a poem, replacing what would have been the reading for the day, the account of the Circumcision of Jesus (See below, p. 45-47), with a personal reflection on what the beginning of a new year represents, a recollection of the past, with its mixture of joy and sorrow, and the hope for the future. The first poem thus marks the start of the secular year, not the religious year, but it nevertheless adopts the questioning tone which will reverberate throughout the cycle.

She employs a familiar device, known to the Middle Ages as well as to the 16th and 17th Centuries and her own age, of a dialogue between the human heart and, in this case, the New Year. The heart is afraid: the prospect of a joyful future is offered, but there is not, and rarely will be, any indication that it will become a reality. The doubts and inconclusiveness of the whole cycle are there from the beginning.

On New Year's Day

My eyes are closing, my senses are about to leave me.
"Fare well, Old Year, with joy and sorrow!
Heaven will bestow a new one, if it so desires."
Thus does man incline his head towards the goodness of God.
The old blossom falls, the new one is sprouting, silently,
out of ice and snow, God's plant.

Night is fleeing, sleep from my eye-lids:
"Welcome, young day, with your brethren!
Where are you then, beloved New Year?"
There it is in the splendour of the morning light.
The whole earth has embraced it
and gazes earnestly and clearly into its eyes.

"Greetings to you, human heart with all your frailty,
you heart full of power and regret and pain,
I bring you from the Lord a new time of trial."
"Greetings to you, New Year, with all your joys.
Life is so sweet and - ah! - one accepts everything,
even suffering, willingly along with life."

"Oh, human heart, how has your house collapsed!
How can you, heir to those halls,
how can you live in such desolate horror?"
"Oh New Year, to be sure I am never at home.
A wanderer, I traverse distant spaces.
It may be called my house, yet it is not."

"Oh, human heart, what have you to do
that you cannot remain in your homeland
and keep it in readiness for your Lord?"
"Oh, New Year, you have much to learn.
Do you not know war and pestilence and perils?
And my dearest cares dwell far away."

"O human heart, can you compel everything then?
Must heaven bring you dew and rain?

And does the earth open itself to your word?"
"Ah, no, I can but see and be sad.
Things have remained, alas, as they were,
and continue along the given paths."

"Oh wily heart! You simply do not wish to say it.
The world has set up her tents
And refreshes you in them with her dizzy wine."
"That bitter goblet cannot bring me joy.
Its foam means sin and its liquid means remorse,
and sorrow never leaves me alone either."

"Listen, oh heart, I want to explain it to you.
Do you want to bind the arrow in its flight?
You do not see its target. Does that mean it has none?"
"I know indeed that a day is prepared for us,
and then it will be clear that all has turned out well
and all the thousand goals are nevertheless one."

"Oh heart, you are completely gripped by foolishness.
You know all this, and can you still be afraid?
Oh, wicked servant, faithless to all duty!
Each thing fulfils its role with honour,
goes its way and never allows itself to be disturbed.
Thy likeness does not exist on earth.

You have wickedly banished peace.
Yet the grace of God is endless, like His love.
Oh come home to your desolate house!
Come back into your dark and barren cell,
and wash it clean with your tears,
and breathe fresh air into it with your sighs

And if you wish, faithfully, to cast your gaze upwards,
then the Lord will send His holy image to you,
to treasure it in faith and trust.
Then some time I may entwine myself upon your garland,
and if the New Year were yet to find you,
may it gaze into a little house of God."

On the Feast of Epiphany

In this case, although she does not head the poem with the biblical reference, she evokes the familiar factual account of the journey of the Magi, as related briefly by St Matthew but taken up time and again by succeeding generations attracted by its momentous significance in the story of the Nativity. She begins with a colourful, dramatic description of her own, as she imagines the Three Kings, with their entourage, making their way through the night. The later Droste-Hülshoff would excel at descriptions of natural settings and the evocation of atmosphere, in her epics and her prose writings as well as in some of her great lyric poems, but already here the young poet succeeds in describing vividly the setting for this famous journey. Colour and light mix with the darkness, and a single sound, the clinking of the trappings on the dromedaries, cuts through the prevailing silence.

However, the poem is much more than a description of a familiar scene. She is making a more profound point, moving from the description of the Magi following the star to her own journey towards the light. As early as this, there is evidence of her confusion, and her despair of finding her way. As so often, as the cycle proceeds, the transition in her thought is not obvious, though she makes it seem so. The journey for her soul, as for the three Wise Men, is fraught with peril, yet faith is the guiding force for them, and, she implies, she clings to the thought that it will be for her, too.

Three travellers make their way through the night,
with purple bands about their foreheads,
and burnt from the hot winds and the trials of the long journey.
At a distance the host of servants follows
through the rustling green of the palm trees.

Golden jewels gleam
from the flanks of the dromedaries,
as they step forward with a clinking sound,
and sweet fragrances waft through the air.

Darkness, black and dense, conceals
whatever that region contains.
The figures threaten like giants:
travellers, are you not afraid?
Yet even though the meadow of clouds
weaves a thousand veils, loosely and lightly,
a twinkling little star breaks
triumphantly through the fragile grey.
Slowly it swirls through the blueness
and the procession follows its light.

Listen, the servants whisper softly:
is the town not yet ready to appear,
with its temples and its glades,
the town which is the reward for so much effort?
Even if the desert were burning hot,
even if vipers were coiling around us,
or tigers pursuing us,
even if the fiery wind were drying up our sweat,
our eyes are fixed on the gifts
for the King strong and wise.

Without anxiety, without concern,
the three make their way through the night,
like three silent moons around the glow of the sun.
When the avalanche of dust cracks,
when the flowers of the desert stretch out
with their terrible yet beautiful spots, (f)
they gaze in silence at that power
which will surely cover them,
which has fanned the star into life.

Oh, you lofty, holy threesome!
Born in darkness, hardly a ray has picked you out,
and yet you follow so piously and so faithfully.

And you, my soul, revelling freely
in the waves of grace,
drawn with force towards the light,
you seek anew the darkness.
Oh, how have you deceived yourself!
For you remained tears, and remorse.

And yet, my soul, take courage,
even if you cannot ever fathom
how you can find forgiveness:
God is good above all things.
Even if in the flood of remorse
you have rescued yourself from the crowd,
although it may burn you to the marrow,
seething in secret fire,
He who wooed you with His blood
never abandons you to the throng.

I am not worthy of a ray,
not the smallest light from above.
Lord, I will praise Thee joyfully,
whatever Thy will grants to me.
Be it suffering that consumes me,
should I lose that which is dearest to me,
should I detect no consolation,
should no prayer of mine be heard:
if it can but lead me to Thee,
then, flame and sword, be welcome!

(f) She is apparently referring to snakes, as in her novel *Ledwina*. See Woesler, IV, 2, p 327.

On the First Sunday after Epiphany
Luke 2, 42-52: Jesus teaches in the temple

The text for this poem relates the episode when Jesus, at the age of twelve, is left behind in Jerusalem and discovered only three days later when His parents find Him in the temple among the teachers, listening to them and answering their questions. From this familiar story, Droste-Hülshoff takes just the words of Christ's anxious mother, as she reproaches Him for causing such anxiety to herself and Joseph. The Authorized Version has 'Thy father and I have sought thee <u>sorrowing</u>!', but she uses the same phrase as Luther, 'mit Schmerzen' - 'in pain'- and the words become the pivotal expression of her own anguished search for God. This theme, so important throughout the cycle, frames the poem, with the opening words repeated in the final line, but then with the desperate plea that God should not hide Himself from her. Another single line stands out, with the desperate statement in the penultimate strophe: "I know that Thou existeth, but I must feel it, too." The young woman is struggling, as she will do throughout her life, with the tension between knowledge and feeling, and the relationship of both with the faith she recognized in her step-grandmother but could no longer find in herself.

> Behold! I have sought Thee in anguish.
> My Lord and my God, where shall I find Thee?
> Ah, not in my own deserted heart,
> where long ago Thy image was extinguished in sin.
> Then, from all corners, if I call Thee,
> my own echo resounds around me like mockery.
>
> If anyone has ever lost Thy godly image
> that belonged to him like his soul,
> with that person has the whole world conspired
> in order to conceal Thy holy countenance from him.
> And where the pious man sees Thee on Mount Tabor,
> there in the valley has he built his house.
>
> Thus to my horror I must come to know
> the puzzle that I could never solve,
> when in the bright years of my innocence

that which was evil there seemed quite incomprehensible to me:
that a soul in which Thy image has shone
no longer recognizes Thee when it sees Thee.
All around me sounds the clear singing of the birds:
"Listen: the little birds are singing His praise!"
And I wish to bend towards a flower and say
"His gentle eye looks out from every flower."
I have sought Thee in Nature,
and worldly knowledge was the only fruit.

And I must gaze into the passage of fate,
as a good heart often in this life
in vain steps towards Thee out of its forward march,
until, despairing, it has yielded to sin
Then all love seems to me like mockery,
and I perceive no mercy, and no God.

And the knots plait themselves so wondrously together
that Thou appearest in light to the faithful gaze.
Then the evil one has stretched out his hand
and builds a bridge of fog to doubt,
and my intellect, which only trusts itself,
believes for sure that it is made of gold.

I know that Thou existeth, but I must feel it, too,
and feel that a cold and heavy hand presses me,
that one day there must be a dark end to these games,
that every deed must pluck its fruit.
I feel that I am offered up to vengeance.
I perceive Thee, yet not joyfully.

Where can I find Thee, in hope and loving?
For that sombre power that I have discerned
is but the shadow that has remained to me
of Thy image, when I had lost it.
Oh God, Thou art so gentle and so radiant.
I seek Thee in anguish: do not conceal Thyself!

On the feast day of the sweet name of Jesus
The Circumcision of Christ

The text which inspired this poem is *Luke* 2, 21. The circumcision of a child occurred traditionally eight days after his birth, and in the Church calendar this would have been the reading for New Year's Day, which, as seen above, Droste-Hülshoff marked instead with a personal reflection at the turn of the year.

Clemens Heselhaus, an eminent interpreter of Droste-Hülshoff, sees this poem, quite rightly, as the product of the pious literary circle in which the young Annette spent much of her time at this point (1959, p.89). Its intention is didactic, and its tone reminiscent of the religious folksong, with the questions and answers that begin each strophe and the frequent repetitions. There is a lightness of touch and a swift movement which she largely rejects in subsequent poems, while the address to 'dear Jesus mine' recalls the personal relationship with Christ familiar from poems in German of the Baroque era. One can assume that it will have pleased her intimate family circle, though the final strophe – and the significant change she made at a later date – betray the darker thoughts much more characteristic of the cycle as a whole.

> What is as sweet as honey
> when it pours out of the comb?
> Sweeter is the seed of life
> which flows through our veins.
> Yet Thy name, dear Jesus mine,
> is gentle and sweet above all things,
> so that death forgets the bitter pain
> when pious lips pronounce it.
> What is equal to the strength of the lion,
> as it prowls round the woods?
> Stronger is passion,
> is the untamed spirit.

Yet Thy name, dear Jesus mine,
is full of power above all things,
so that it crushes into a gentle radiance
that which threatens the world with splendid flames.

What is as rich as the sea-voyage,
like the golden protection of a shaft of light?
Richer is he who preserves for himself
the costly substance of his honour.
Yet Thy name, dear Jesus mine,
is greater and richer than all of that.
Ah, for its sake one endures quite alone
shame, rejection, the loss of all honour.

What is as lovely as the morning light,
like the starry vaulting of the night?
Ah, a sweet countenance
and in the eyes a splendid spirit.
Yet Thy name, dear Jesus mine,
is gentle and lovely above all things.
He who carries it in his tranquil face
is blessed, whatever nature has bestowed upon him.

What is so joyful as to go forth
into the fertile world?
Ah, much more joyful that from which we flee,
the unrecognized family home.
Yet Thy name, dear Jesus mine,
is full of ecstasy above all things.
Oh, who would not for the sake of his joys
give up home and freedom, all that is known to him?

Yes, Thy name, Jesus Christ,
is strong and rich and gentle,
and he who never forgets that name
knows the protection against all suffering.
And I, dearest Jesus mine,
I wretched one, (f) faithless to all duty,
am even so the heir to Thy name.
God: Thou desirest not the death of the sinner.

(f) When she returned to this poem at a much later stage (1838), she changed the adjective 'versunken' to 'arm' ('poor') in the last line but two of the final strophe, realizing that the stark alternative which was her early thought would cause shock and grief to those close to her, suggesting that she was sunk beyond hope. It may have represented her thinking at the time, but the second version suggests that she has mellowed somewhat in the meantime.

On the Third Sunday after Epiphany
Matthew 8, 1-13: of the Leper and the Centurion

For this early confrontation with her guilt and her anguished desire for faith, Droste-Hülshoff uses the story of Christ's healing, first of the leper, and then of the centurion's servant. The words with which she opens the poem echo the injunction reported by St Matthew in both instances: the cure asked for follows as the reward for faith. The message is clear: Jesus is merciful to those who believe. Droste-Hülshoff recognizes this but is tormented by her own uncertain hold on faith. The poem is laden with words and imagery which speak of her sense of being excluded, in the darkness, crying out for the gentleness which she knows to be available to her and yet which still eludes her. It speaks of her state of mind at this stage and accounts for her decision not to proceed with the original plan of presenting these poems to her step-grandmother. It may also explain in some measure why she decided to abandon the project at this point.

> Go forth, and may it befall you as you have believed!
> Yes, whosoever believes, to him will good fortune occur.
> But what to him whom life has robbed
> of its holiness in hidden pangs?

> Lord, speak one word, and Thy servant will be restored to health.
> Lord, speak that word: I can but wish for it.
> The heart can joyfully bestow upon you love,
> but faith reveals itself only as a grace.

How does it come about that when I cried to you in the evening
and when in the morning I went forth to find you,
Thou didst allow me to sink into half-heartedness
and the sin of despair, deeply and ever deeper?

Did not my cry in my greatest anguish
rise up to you out of the depths?
And did it not seem as if I were crying out to the cliffs,
when all the while my eyes were red with tears?

Oh Lord, forgive that which is spoken out of anguish,
for I have sensed Thee often and sweetly.
Indeed, I was at one with Thee for hours on end,
and in my torment I did not remember this.

And now it seems to me as if I, all alone,
were banished from Thy vast banquet of grace,
the beggar shut out before the gates.
Yet, oh God, the guilt is surely mine!

Did I not feel in my humility, worthless as I am,
that I have received Thy word in my spirit,
that my sighs have reached Thy ears,
that my soul recognizes Thee and reveres Thee?

My Lord, think not of my sins!
How often, on the path that I have chosen for myself,
have I cried out, God, in the darkness, for Thy mercy,
as for a right and for an obligation!

Ah, if only I had not neglected those gifts,
if only I had not trodden them underfoot, and despised them!
Then I would not be standing so terribly deranged,
as though the light now flown had been a dream.

How often, even before the deed came to pass
which as a thought had flown around me greedily,
did Thy name pass silently past me in gentle admonition,
Thy image on Golgotha.

And if now, recklessly, I have turned aside,
committed that sin which I have clearly acknowledged,
how hast Thou then in remorseful longing
not often burnt within my soul!

Alas, I have committed many grievous sins,
and still more errors, slight to mention
yet great in the depth of destruction they can sow,
deaf for the sound of the wailing conscience.

Now at last all light has passed away from me,
and often Thy voice has completely died away.
Yet do not cast me – Thou seest that I am still able to desire –
among the dead, for I am alive.

My Jesus, see, I am wounded unto death
and in my broken state I cannot be well again.
My Jesus, think of Thine own bitter wounds
and speak one word; then Thy servant will be cured.

On the Fourth Sunday after Epiphany
Matthew 20, 1-16: The Labourers in the Vineyard

The parable of the labourers in the vineyard is itself quite
problematic, but the way in which Droste-Hülshoff uses it means
that this poem is many-layered and one of the more complex of her
early contributions to *Das Geistliche Jahr*. The echo of the story as
related by St Matthew is there, in the second line, but the plural
'Niemand hat uns gedingt' ('No-one has hired us') is replaced by
the singular 'Keiner hat mich gedingt', for this is a very personal
statement, which immediately moves into a theme which concerns
her in many of her poems, her sense of the gift of poetry and her
duty to use it well. Already she is tormented by her belief that she

has betrayed this gift and that, though chosen by God, she will have to answer on the Day of Judgment for allowing the powers He has bestowed upon her 'to perish in muddy ground'.

As so often, she is harsh in her judgment of herself, but her poem, like the parable, concludes with the awareness of the Love of God. The master in the Gospel story is gentle in his treatment of the servants, not discriminating against those who came late and did not do the full day's work completed by the first to be hired in the morning. Nor is he harsh in his reprimand to those who object that they are given only the same payment as the late-comers. Although the penultimate strophe shows Droste-Hülshoff overwhelmed by her sense of her dejection, 'quite impoverished and in rags' and plunged into the very depths, the redeeming power of remorse surmounts this, with the final reference to the 'gentle spirit' and the emphasis on Love.

I cannot say:
"No one has hired me".
To whom shall I complain
if I am forced downwards
into the bonds which shamefully I myself have woven?
Thou hast chosen me from among millions,
hast paid me in addition untold sums
in the sacred pledge of Thy baptism.

I cannot say:
"Behold, I have borne
the burden of the day."
If now my feeble sun,
paled into vapour, wishes to abandon me,
my garden lies like a moor covered in green,
and the will-o-the wisp rises dazzlingly out of it,
leading the wanderer, the drenched one, into death.

CHAPTER FIVE

I cannot say:
"Behold, who stood by me?
I had to be afraid,
around me the wilderness
and the wild animals which do not recognize Thee at all."
Ah God, to join me in my labours,
Thou hast placed many dear souls around me,
in whom Thy name burns and cannot be extinguished.

I cannot say:
"Behold, Thy voice has spoken.
I had to be bold,
and my strength failed.
Why hast Thou deprived me of my nourishment?"
My God, even if it lies deep in my breast,
I am even so aware of great powers,
and in my fear I have deceived myself.

I must vanish
into the deepest abyss,
dissipate in the breezes
like the vapour from a cloud,
when Thy judgment stands before my spirit.
Thou hast appointed me over many things,
and I appear quite impoverished and in rags.
I have allowed Thy lands to perish in muddy ground.

I can say nothing,
for my hand is empty.
Shall I venture
to weigh the late impulses
of my remorse heavy in the scale?
And if it resembles nothing but the mockery of a substitute,
then I have nothing else. Yet Thou - ah gentle God! –
Thou hast a great, great word of Love.

On the Feast of the Purification of the Virgin Mary (Candlemas)

St Luke (2, 22-40) relates how Mary and Joseph made the traditional visit to the temple forty days after the birth of the Child Jesus, when, according to Jewish law, male children must be presented and thanks given to God, and when the mother must also present herself for purification before God. This ceremony, celebrated on 2 February, has always been seen in the Christian Church as the end of the Christmas season, when candles are brought into the churches for blessing; hence the name 'Candlemas' in English and 'Lichtmeß' in German.

There are two distinct aspects of Droste-Hülshoff's poem. On the one hand she presents a tender picture of the woman cradling her child, setting aside at this point the extraordinary circumstances of His birth, and of Joseph, solicitous for the welfare of the Mother and Child as he walks by her side, and, at the end, gently pulls her cloak around her to shield her from the hot sun, before resuming what he knows to be his proper place behind the Holy Pair. Between these two vignettes, accentuated in the last two strophes in the repetition of words and phrases from the opening strophes, lies the less visual central section of the poem, in which Droste-Hülshoff writes much more characteristically of her torment as she contemplates the tiny Child, the Son of God, and expresses her awe in His presence and her awareness of her inner conflicts, torn between an inadequate faith and an overwhelming love. Yet, even so, she feels more able to address Him, distant as she knows Him to be, than to turn to Mary, the traditional intermediary between Christ and the human sinner. With Mary she shares her human form and her womanhood, but she expresses her inhibitions about attempting to communicate with the immaculate Virgin, whose very perfection seems to make her inaccessible to her, an idea which ran counter to the teaching of the Church and may have caused surprise, even shock, among those who read this at the time.

At this point in her life she was racked with guilt and self-accusation, and we know that the poem, as it stands here in something like a final version, had undergone some drastic changes, when she rejected several of the original strophes which she realized were too stark to inflict on her nearest and dearest and replaced them with a softer tone. We know, too, that she revised this poem in some haste, in order to send it to her mother, and this fact may well account for the difficulty of its syntax, particularly in the central part. It remains, however, as a tender picture of the Holy Family, and as an indication of her allegiance to the values in which she had been brought up, even though at this point she was tussling with them and would do so increasingly throughout her life.

The place of the Virgin Mary in the religious thinking of the young Droste-Hülshoff, an important place in the conventional teaching within her family circle, probably accounts for the fact that she devotes two of the poems of the first part of *Das Geistliche Jahr* to her feast days; this one and the later one marking the Annunciation (see below, pp.80-82), yet none to the available occasions of the later part of the year. There is no poem for the Assumption of the Virgin (15 August), or for the days traditionally dedicated to her birth (8 September) or the day of her naming (15 September). It is possible that the older Droste-Hülshoff had less firm a hold, in this respect as in so many others, on the simpler, more pious thinking of her early education, and one can even see in this very early poem a movement away from it, with the rejection of the idea that Mary is the natural confidante of sinful man and the idea that the Son of God, in the form of the little child, is so far above her that she can appeal to Him more easily and with all possible comparison removed. The young poet is already displaying the independence of mind which disturbed her and which so characterised her later development.

Mary passes through the little streets,
in her arms her Son, the dear One,
holds him tightly, holds him gently,
and she gazes down at Him.
How the cherubs sang of Him,
how the shepherds worshipped Him
and the grey-haired Wise Men paid homage:
all that she allows to pass her by in silence.

But at her side Joseph is
quite caught up in care.
Testing, he asks all the stones
if her foot steps too firmly.
He does not know what he will experience,
but wondrous things
have secretly announced themselves to him
out of the eyes of the little Child.

Oh Mary, Mother of Christ,
I will not dare to approach you,
for you are too radiant for me.
My soul grows fearful in your presence.
You almost terrify me
in the immaculate purity
which you triumphantly preserved
when you walked as I do now.

I will much rather go before your little Child,
weeping and dejected.
He is my Lord and my Judge indeed,

whereas you are not so far away from me.
I must pay the price of a foolish deed,
if I am not to disintegrate in fear,
since, after all, has He not conquered,
is He not the hero of eternity?

Dearest Lord, Thou hast created
my poor sick soul,
like that many-faceted lure
that guides us on broad roads,
and Thou knowest that just as before others
fresh breath within my soul
touches me with its glow
so also before others does every earthly joy.

Thou hast bestowed upon me
side by side with abundant powers
the splendid task of ruling over wealthy estates,
and a lofty, rich castle.
And now it lies in ruins,
terrible in its barren immensity,
like a monster turned to bone,
like a dead giant of the ocean.

And when, after many days,
devoid of faith but full of love,
I anxiously tested its walls,
behold, they stood firm!
Oh, my Lord, if Thou wilt hear me,
and open up the treasures of Thy grace,
behold, I will faithfully build
the wretched remnants of my life.

And even though my house must stand,
a barren, threatening ruin,
alas, only there can that which was destroyed
so completely without hope reconstruct itself
and I can build just a little room,
adorned with silent deeds, where, Lord, I can entertain
Thee as my guest, when Thou comest to me.

Mary steps out of the halls,
in her arms her Son, the dear One,
holds Him firmly, holds him gently,
and her eyes rest upon Him.
Ah, she has borne this joy
for nine blissful months.
That which those pious ones announced,
she carried for a long time in her radiant spirit.

But Joseph no longer walks with silent steps
by her side,
for the dear, dear little Child
is now the Lord of the whole world.
Yet, as the sun climbs higher,
he slips softly behind her
and pulls her cloak
so that her veil drops down.

On the Fifth Sunday after Epiphany
Of the seed which fell among thorns

The familiar parable of the sower who went out to sow his seeds is
related in three of the Gospels, explicitly here that of Luke (8, 7-
14), which, with the question from the disciples as to its meaning
and the interpretation which Jesus gives to them, is the starting-
point for Droste-Hülshoff in this poem, which needs little
elucidation within the context of her religious poems and of her
spiritual journey. It does, however, show the fluidity in her use of
the Gospel texts, and it is probably one of the most effective of the
early poems.

Familiar features are there: the feeling of her closeness to God,
yet her anguish and her constant doubt, her sense of being
mistakenly perceived by other people, of waging a constant battle

with herself and with the gentler instincts which draw her to the absolute faith that eludes her.

She uses both the Gospel narrative and other familiar motifs with great power and clarity. The thorns are the thorns of her bitter remorse, but, where the parable speaks of them as stifling the Word of God, here they protect it and allow it to flourish, but it is she herself, the soil into which it falls, which is too hard to receive and nurture it. In the third strophe, the thorns are linked with a garland, her head, and, above all, with searing pain: the echo of the Crucifixion is there and underlines the prevailing sense of agony. The devil lurks, filling her with trembling fear and threatening her with his wiles, yet also prompting her to fight against him. Always she seeks redemption and hopes for the bright day of joy while fearing that it will always elude her, in this world and the next.

Thy Word has fallen among the thorns,
thorns which have torn my heart to pieces.
Thou, my God, only Thou alone canst know
that they are painful above all others:
into the thorns of my bitter remorse
which will not yet receive consolation.
Thus I concealed it in dark awe,
and thus it grew up in sadness.

And so it grows up in bitter joy,
and the thorns allow it to thrive.
Alas, my soil is too hard, and in the open air
the sun licks from it the dew from the cliff.
Even so it can unfold but slowly,
though they faithfully protect it from the storms
and from the breath of desire, cold as death,
and whenever the clouds of doubt tower up.

Thy Word has fallen among the thorns,
and they will bring forth roses soaked in blood.
If I am to venture just once to trust Thee,
I need only swirl in their garland.
When it glows forth in its fiery rays,
and my head burns with deep wounds,
then God's tender plant will flourish
and must be healed in the radiance of His anguish.

Then my life must vanish in resignation
and my time die away in contemplation.
Only thus can I strive for the ultimate.
I must not lift up my eyes.
Alas, I have misused them for sinful purposes,
and frittered away the pure joy of seeing.
Only then can I yet find heaven,
When I refrain from looking at it in shame.

When I gaze upon the gentle features
– alas, how painfully it must afflict me! –
those to whom remains the cherished right
to serve their God in joyfulness,
here too I must direct my sorrowful eyes,
must, glowing, cast them to the ground,
to sink them into a pure eye,
this I can never do without committing a crime.

And however low I bow my sad forehead,
when the sin goes raging past me,
many people believe that it is revulsion that motivates me,
and they love me more and more,
yet often it is only my past life,
terribly born for a second time.
Alas, and I often sense tremblingly
that the Dark One has never lost a game.

Yet, no matter what tricks he harbours,
I will fight for the boundaries of heaven.
My eyes shall gleam with joy
when I lay myself among my thorns,

so that the world may not criticise my battle,
or even accompany it with false praise.
To be sure, I can triumph through God's miracle,
but never fight against two enemies.

Will a day ever dawn on earth for me
when I can openly count myself as one of Thine,
when no sword will ever again penetrate my soul
and when Thy hands will become visible to me?
Lord, and if that day is never to dawn for me,
if I might not hope for it in eternity,
I must nevertheless weep for my sins.
Ah, the sinner has met himself!

Shrove Tuesday

From the Gospel reading for Shrove Tuesday (*Luke* 18,31-43),
Droste-Hülshoff takes the plea of the blind man as Christ journeys
towards Jericho and, opening her poem with it, and repeating it at
the end of each strophe, she creates this statement of her longing
for faith in the midst of the doubt she expresses so often. Once more
she is concerned with the tension between feeling and believing
that she can glimpse the faith she so desires, and the knowledge
that it is there for her. Physical sight is equated with that faith, and
the force of the poem lies in her repetition of the simple appeal to
God, 'Lord, grant that I may see!'

Lord, grant that I may see!
I know that day has dawned,
five blood-red suns are standing in the radiant East,
and that the dawn is reflected with silent glittering
in the bright springs of the heart.
I do not see that it is near, and yet I feel it.
Lord, grant that I may see!

And as I stand alone,
all around me there ring out many different sounds.
Each one wishes to find a bright spot,
and everyone is singing of the joy of the sun.
I can never fathom the splendour,
and all I have is unfathomable pain.
Lord, grant that I may see!

How I do turn my eyes,
yearning though the vast realms of the air,
yet believe that a shimmer of light must fall
into the barren pallor of their wretched circles,
since after all Thy rays are more powerful than all others.
Yet the tough outer crust closes itself more tightly.
Lord, grant that I may see!

Like the deer that has been shot
I should like to run through the world in search of help,
yet I can never find Thy paths.
I know that I shall sink into the moor,
if the wolf does not first swallow up the blind one.
And the steep cliff of pride is threatening, too.
Lord, grant that I may see!

And so I remain upon the peak,
where to protect Thy people Thou hast drawn about them
the tender celestial hall of pious faith
in which the red suns shine so clearly,
and I wait until Thy dew falls from heaven,
in which I may warm my feeble eyes.
Lord, grant that I may see!

However the night may swell up
as if I had formed an alliance with her black power,
because the floods of Thy rays are closed to me,
yet even so their closeness has announced itself to me,
and I do sense that their glow is gentle.
Thus do I know that I do not beg in vain.

Lord, grant that I may see!
And though many may disdain me
as if I were never to arrive at Thy radiance
while I myself am to blame for my blindness,
since through the ostentatious glitter of my powers
I have endured a terribly blinding, fiery light,
let it be right for me, and let him who sows, reap.
Lord, grant that I may see!

Lord, let it come to pass as Thou desirest!
Yet I will never turn from Thy countenance.
In these days when Night is reigning
I will stand alone in Thy temple,
untouched by her cold sceptre,
and see if I can glimpse the spark of Thy grace.
Lord, grant that I may see!

I feel that Thy radiance is blowing all about me,
in all my limbs,
which stir in fearful longing.
O, gentle Lord, look down with pity.
Can an endless pleading not move Thee?
Even if the cock crows a third time,
Lord, grant that I may see!

On Ash Wednesday

For this poem Droste-Hülshoff concentrates not on a specific text, but on the single symbol of the day in the Catholic Church, the cross made in ash on the forehead of believers. The primary significance of the ash is penance, but she intertwines it also throughout the poem with the familiar notion of man as dust and ashes, and she borrows – perhaps almost instinctively - both this theme and much of her vocabulary and imagery from Baroque poetry and even, notably in the first strophe, from the medieval idea of the world as corrupting and deceiving with its superficial

beauty and colour. The reality of death, so allied to the meaning
of Ash Wednesday, is contrasted with the frivolity of the waste of
life, with its ephemeral values. The second half of the poem
becomes, as so often, much more personal, with the familiar self-
accusation and tortured appeals to God for forgiveness, while the
poem closes with the juxtaposition of the immortal soul and the
transitory human body. The phrase 'intellect and understanding'
in the fourth strophe will become a familiar concern in her poems,
as she speaks of the conflict within her of mind and heart, of
knowledge and belief: already here she sees cerebral activity as
bringing only pain.

> Upon my brow this Cross,
> grey with ash!
> O, contemptible worldly attractions,
> how cunningly
> you deceive us!
> You strew the mouldy ground
> with bright and vivid colours,
> red and white.
> Then Death comes along
> and gives the lie to you.
>
> And then he who has not thought it through
> and really known it
> must weep, he who has laughed away
> his life
> in vain pleasure.
> He pays no heed to what is dear to him,
> and that which is valuable to him
> flees from him like a thief,
> drops to the ground and into bones.
>
> So what is it that adorns itself
> in colourful silk?
> What walks about in gold and pearls?

Oh Lord, I grasp
at all that is not good,
at illusion and dream
and hang earth and blood
and the foam of the sea round
brightly-coloured ash.

What is so passionately loved?
What places in chains intellect and understanding,
even if it yields nothing but pain?
Oh Lord, forgive me!
One does not love the soul,
the noble bride,
and about a face, formed out of dust,
one wafts
eternal remorse.

If a skeleton appears
before my eyes,
my hair stands on end,
and I recoil before
that which I am and shall remain,
and know already
yet bear it myself
to bitter scorn
in my own body.

If I feel the pulse beat
in my hand,
what do I think about?
O empty nothingness, if I recover!
And do not in madness think that
again and again
each pulse beat consumes
my life,
inflicting mortal wounds.

You despicable body
that often leads me astray,
touches my heart deeply

with the world and with sin,
you are still alive.
Soon you will lie rigid as ice,
mocked by the worms,
surrendered to the elements.
Ah, may God
raise up my soul!

On the First Sunday in Lent
The Temptation of Christ

Droste-Hülshoff uses the scene of the temptation of Christ in the
wilderness, and the threefold mocking injunction of the devil, to
open another poem which speaks very powerfully of her own
anguished search for faith. Once more the young girl is racked with
guilt and accusing herself of inadequacies and misdemeanours
surely inconceivable in one of her youth and background, and
showing, some would say, how profoundly the unfortunate episode
with Straube and Arnswaldt had affected her. For the first time in
the cycle, she faces death in terror, though all the time clinging to
her belief in a merciful God.

"Command that these stones become bread!
Let your angels carry you down!
Behold the kingdoms of all this world!
Will you not renounce your creator?"
Dark spirit, you were completely misguided
to tempt your Lord and your God.
Alas, countless numbers hang in your nets,
lost because of the treacherous fruit.

Ambition, pride, the pleasures of this world,
idols for whom precious souls die.
Ah, my God, let me not depart for ever!
Let me not myself attain death.

CHAPTER FIVE

Quite confused, I do not know how to hold myself in check.
Threatening, the false ground sways about me.
Alas, relying on my own weak strength,
I step unthinking into the gaping abyss.

My Jesus, my prayers rise up to Thee,
my voice upon the ladder of the Cross.
Thou touchest the seas and they vanish,
and the mountains smoulder at Thy rage.
And yet Thy unending words of mercy blossom
upwards with a thousand heavenly branches.
"Thou dost not extinguish the candle that glimmers,
nor dost Thou break the bent reed." (f)

Lord, I am a poor and barely glimmering little candle
on the altar of Thy Grace.
Behold, a gentle passing breeze extinguishes me
like a droplet from the earth's shore.
Alas, if just a single little point of light
did not remain within my heart,
that hot spark of Thy love,
how completely dead would I be in that case!

Lord, Thou hast ordained perhaps much more
for this brief, restless life,
whether I am to be poured away in torment,
whether I should weave in every joy.
If I may choose, and if rapture will part from me,
burn me in the pure flames of suffering.
Alas, despair teaches me to speak Thy name,
and yet honour is so glad to stand alone.

Is there perhaps lurking hidden in the praise
that people offer me a high point,
so that I may still have the last scrap of strength
to laud Thee and to sing Thy praises?
And are the nets spread out here
so that lips may labour in honour of Thee,
and might I be too weak to bear that praise,
and might it break my only remaining strength?

Lord, Thou knowest how wretchedly in my soul,
how lost the prayers are,
so that I might wish to atone
as though for great transgressions and dare to plead for that.
My prayer is like the prayer of a dead man,
is a cold mist before Thy throne.
Lord, Thou hast Thyself offered it to me,
and Thou didst listen to the Prodigal Son.

Lord, deep though I may have sunk among all people,
let me feel it for ever more.
Let me not, to add to all my sins,
fall also into wanton foolishness.
My duties stand above many things,
and among all things the power of my virtue.
Alas, I must surely squander my strength
in the game of sin and passion.

If Thou dost wish to bestow more earthly things,
and I must lose those I possess,
then let me be mindful in joy and misery
of what is owing to poor strangers.
If I carry all earthly fortunes to the grave,
it will perhaps remain immortal for me if by sacrificing
I divide up my poor substance faithfully.

I cannot venture to fight this battle myself.
I have lost all Thy mercies,
If Thou dost abandon me,
I cannot complain
since after all I have chosen the dark:
pride, ambition, the delights of this world.
Oh, my Jesus, draw me back!
What must I do to avoid them,
other than turn my frightened gaze towards Thee?

(f) *Isaiah* 42, 3: 'A bruised reed shall he not break, and the smoking flax shall he not quench.' The words are repeated in *Matthew* 12,20, with the additional '…till he send forth judgment unto victory.' Droste-Hülshoff takes up the reference in the next strophe of her poem, when she speaks of herself as the 'poor and barely glimmering little candle'.

On the Second Sunday in Lent

The account of the meeting of Jesus with the woman of Canaan (*Matthew* 15, 21-28) raises some puzzling issues: Christ seems to reject her, not just the once when He tells her to go away since she is a Gentile and He has come 'but unto the lost sheep of the house of Israel', but again, apparently more ruthlessly, by likening her to a dog, in an image certainly known to her and the other listeners and appearing to reflect the contempt in which non-Jews were held by Jews. The encounter is interpreted very differently, however, since Christ responds to the resilience of the woman with compassion: He sees her faith in Him and her daughter is cured. This, it is traditionally held, is Jesus teaching the value of prayer and belief, and this is how Droste-Hülshoff uses the Gospel message, but, with characteristic originality and pungency, taking up first the idea of a little dog, searching for the 'crumbs that fall'. That idea gives way later in the poem, however, to the pursuit of what these crumbs will be, the faith which she so desires and the search for which will accompany her all her life.

Dearest Jesus, only patience!
Like a little dog I will hunt
after the crumbs of Thy Grace,
will settle down in front of the doors,
to see whether one of Thy children will not
offer me a little crust,
glowing with hunger yet silent
in the knowledge of my profound misery.

I beseech Thee for patience,
for I must lie lonely
before the door in great anguish,
when the fragrance of Thy pure weeping,
of Thy gifts with all the freshness of life,
passes over me.

Ah, a single drop can refresh me;
my tongue has burnt itself out.

Because in my anguish
I look out almost with the eyes of a child,
Thy servants often think
that I must rank as a guest.
Boldly in their pity
they hold out the dishes to me,
yet I will not forget
that I am like a little dog.

Ah, I must count it as the utmost blessing
in respect of Thee
that nothing can compare with Thy forbearance,
my one and only that Thou art,
for it often flashes through my limbs
like lightning
to pair myself with Thy children,
quickly finding a place for myself.

And yet, Thou mighty Avenger,
I cannot lie to you in all eternity,
and it would be a shameful fate for me
to deceive Thy servants like this.
Because my eyes burn softly
in unrequited passion,
I shall call myself a little child
with a breast shattered by guilt.

I am only like a little dog,
and so I shall never cease
to follow Thy children
to see if they will offer me a crust.
When the sun has risen in the sky
and when it turns to blood and dies,
I shall hang on their lips
when Thou dost offer them their supper.

If Thy children deem it right
to grant me even a little crust,

then well enough: nothing seems too bad to me
if it comes from gentle hands.
Concealed within it is rich sustenance,
only hardened by earnest heat.
And ah: a stone would not be too hard
for my dulled senses.

Alas, it is a bitter lot
for one who has been a cherished guest
to pick up now the crumbs
for the sake of his own great sins,
not for the rigour of the law,
which still threatens me as once it did,
but in the pressure
of my own profound contemplation.

New senses have been bestowed upon me
around the fire of my longing,
but not while a bond holds
body and soul in its embrace,
and therein lies my only hope.
Thus I slowly live my life.
My senses are receptive,
but sense is lacking in them.

In torment must the dawn behold me,
and the light of evening, too.
Ah, how sweet is death!
And yet I must not dare to plead for its solace,
no matter how it waves and beckons so gently,
for I must atone eternally,
and life is my shield.

On the Third Sunday in Lent
Mark 5, 1-10: Jesus drives out the devil

The poem begins and ends with the dramatic pronouncement by
the devil that his name is Legion, one of many such dark spirits, and

once more Droste-Hülshoff is confronting her own sense of guilt. A new and very significant element enters the cycle at this point, however: her sense of a dichotomy between her religion and her art. She turns in searing accusation towards the sinful sound of her songs, but 'empty of words and deeds. So confused in senses' as she believes herself to be, she can yet trust in the mercy of God. The poem stands in sharp contrast to others where she sees her poetry as a gift to be used in the service of God, not, as here, as a curse which separates her from Him.

"My name is Legion, for there are many of us",
thus spoke the dark spirit.
His name is Legion, woe to me, that I feel it,
that it is causing me to tremble.

When the spirit, like a child's, knows only its Jesus,
in simplicity and trust,
the dark one cannot fashion his tortuous caverns
in that perfectly radiant ground.

Yet you, my guilt-laden heart, with your vain knowledge,
in your misguided doings:
how many thousand burning places have opened up in you,
in which the night can rest?

And if I draw myself up and wish
to brave the sound of the holy name,
ah, could not perhaps my good intention lead
to a new grievous fall?

For it casts me down immeasurably
that the world, the people,
do not know me, I who blaze like the sea,
so that often they still even call me bright and joyful.

The world must know me. I must endure contempt,
such as I have always merited, worm that I am

who dares to praise Him whom the angels
hardly venture to name.

Let me sing of Thee, in remorse and in fear,
my Saviour and my God,
and let the sound of my song not fade away,
this elaborate, sinful sound, an outrage and a mockery.

Alas, the song of one who is, like me, so empty of words and deeds,
so confused in senses,
can only strengthen the Lord's compassionate miracle
and turn it into a blessing.

Is not my whole day but a succession of sins?
Must not desire, awakening,
often find in the illusion of a dream innumerable paths,
but only never the way to heaven?

Does not the battle-song of desire resound from all sides,
and does it not bring victory?
Is not my life but weak and fleeting fighting,
a war covered in shame?

And if I ever believe that I have gained the victory,
because desire has vanished,
then I shall be sucked dry as though by the Empusa, (f)
like a dead hand.

And if there is a time for me when life seems to flow
into a heart completely turned to stone,
then at the same time the exuberance which was waiting
for a breath must lose its fire.

And if at last surrounded by the sparks of suffering,
I recognize how small I am, a nothing,
then am I burnt out, fallen into ashes,
smouldered away in heart and mind.

And you have yourself to thank for that, you guilty heart.
My dear, beloved Jesus:

if you had only remained a little faithful, He
would never have faltered in His love for His bride.

But because, slumbering, you allow the terrible force of hell
to make its way through all the gates
so that on all sides the garlands of victory
blossom for it out of your own soil;

because, poor barren branch, you foolishly delude yourself,
that you are in brightly-coloured leaf,
and because, while the enemy is rejoicing at plundering you,
you believe that you are rich and splendid,

that is why you die, and why in the fire of your delusion,
you do not recognize your own pain.
Ah, if only you could feel yourself bleeding from every vein,
you foolish, wicked heart!

And so behold your anguish! The barriers of dark eternity
have not yet closed.
"His name is Legion": grasp that thought!
Time is running out.

(f) The Empusa, in Greek mythology the daughter of Hecate: she was said to have feasted on the blood of young men she had seduced.

On the Fourth Sunday in Lent
The Feast of St Joseph

St Joseph was highly esteemed in the Catholic Church in the 19th century, with something close to a cult developing around him, in parallel to the much greater adoration of the Virgin Mary, who, by 1854, was the focus of the new dogma of the Immaculate Conception. This status will, of course, have been familiar to Droste-Hülshoff, but it is puzzling that, aware though she must have been that only Mary was deemed to be sinless, she speaks in this poem of the sinfulness of Joseph, a view not emphasised by the Church and one with which Droste-Hülshoff herself may have come to be uneasy. The poem as it stands here is as she wrote it to begin with, though her editors removed several of the strophes which refer to sins and guilt in Joseph when it came to publication, before restoring them in later editions. It may be that she expressed her misgivings to her friends without ever herself removing or changing these references but that this occurred in the course of conversations recalled by them after her death without the evidence of written emendations.

Certainly, the picture offered of Joseph is strangely ambiguous, which can hardly have been her intention and which conflicts with the totally positive and intensely human depiction of him in the poem for Candlemas. The strophes in question are the fifth, the ninth and the tenth, the last two of which imply a reputation for Joseph at odds with prevailing thinking, while the first seems to depend on imagination of what may have been the case but is unsupported by the Gospels. In other respects, the poem extols St Joseph, whose feast day was celebrated with affection and enthusiasm on 19 March and seems to reflect the sentiments of a young woman growing up in a conventional Catholic household in Westphalia at that time. Her paradoxical desire, as it seems, to represent St Joseph as a thoroughly human figure, a prey to doubts and even to faults, may perhaps be compared with the feeling expressed in the poem for Candlemas that the Virgin, precisely because she is human, yet sinless and far above her, is a less appropriate channel for communication than her Child, the Son of God, God Himself.

Welcome to you in your radiance,
you pure evening sun,
you ancient lily branch,
who in your grey days
have yet brought forth
such a gentle wealth of blossoms!

The more they unfold
to form a wreath of honour
that adorns your brow,
the more you bow
your grace-laden head,
inclining low in awe.

How your friendly feast-day
has come to you, my pious one,
into this solemn time!
It was almost as though I were buried
and then you come to soothe me
with rare joyfulness.

I will take refuge with you,
turn my timid life towards you,
oh Joseph, gentle breath!
You have known the flaws
in your strong soul,
have known forgiveness too.

What did you not endure
when Mary, secretly laden with guilt,
appeared before you?
And you could not trust her,
on whom the heavens depend,
and yet you forgave her.

And how great was your distress
when you had to depart
with your two precious ones!
The desert seemed long to you,

and yet your dear Child
was threatened with disaster.

And how little you were mocked
on account of His divine power
when He was crowned in splendour!
How did the wicked priests not abuse you,
in order to assuage their own anger!

And even when pious tongues,
divinely permeated, greeted you
and praised you loudly, far and wide,
how did you not beat your breast
in despair,
in your sinfulness?

Thus you have borne much,
numerous torments,
with friendly patience,
and in all those years
many a sigh has escaped you,
and many a little guilt.

You pious hero; in the faith,
to rob you terribly of which
all the world banded together,
you have not been able to maintain
a spotless rule
at the Hand of your Jesus.

What then shall I not hope,
while heaven is still open
and my soul is silent?
If Grace approaches,
then I can indeed receive it,
if God will help me.

I am torn to the very depths
on account of my sins,

and my remorse is great.
If only I had the confidence
to build my refuge
in the bosom of my Jesus!

On the Fifth Sunday in Lent
John 8, 46-59: The Jews prepare to stone Jesus

Droste-Hülshoff takes the opening words for this poem from the
Gospel for the Fifth Sunday of Lent. St John tells of the
confrontation between Christ and the Jews who challenge Him and
take up stones to cast at Him before He leaves the temple where
they have found Him teaching. In the second strophe, she echoes
the words of the Gospel, when Christ says to His accusers: 'If a man
keep my saying, he shall never taste death.' (v.51) She changes the
formulation significantly, however, and the change is important for
the tone of this poem, which is notably much gentler and more
hopeful than most of the others in this part of the cycle. What she
says is closer to the promise of Jesus to the disciples as reported by
Matthew (10, 39): 'He that loseth his life for my sake shall find it'.
The meaning is very much the same, however, and it gives to the
poem the confidence in the Word of God which shines through her
uncertainty, though, as always, that uncertainty is present, translated
here into the anguish which she acknowledges to be self-inflicted
and which again asserts itself in the central part of the poem.

Something else takes over, however, and the theme of her sense
of vocation as a poet enters the cycle for the first time, though it is
a theme which recurs in her later writings. Her confidence that her
poetry will survive her physical life is expressed with considerable
energy in the seventh strophe, and one cannot help thinking of
her often quoted hope that her work will live long after her death,

perhaps suggesting that it will not be appreciated during her lifetime, as indeed much of it was not (Letter to Elise Rüdiger, 24 July 1843). This very personal note has not surfaced before in *Das Geistliche Jahr* and it has led to the suggestion that this is an intensely autobiographical poem, the result of her friendship with Heinrich Straube and the emotion which it engendered during their meetings in 1819. This explanation would account for the two surprising and seemingly unconnected final strophes, with the sudden address 'My brother...'

The prophets are buried,
Abraham is dead.
Millions, old men and boys,
and rosy maidens,
many who gave me love,
and to whom I gave it:
all of them, they are all buried,
they are all dead.

Lord, Thou hast announced it to me,
and Thy Word stands firm,
that only he finds life
who abandons life.
Alas, it winds its way through my soul,
in dull strained tones;
and yet Thou hast announced it to me,
and Thy Word stands firm.

And yet I often live
in self-inflicted anguish.
All seems well ordained to me,
and only man,
who represents Thy image,
seems to be in misery.
Behold: thus have I inflicted
nameless pain upon myself;

I have sensed with foreboding
how in nature
a nerve hangs only
on a little thread,
how Thy image often vanishes
without a trace:
I have found no spirit,
only a physical body.

Then I see fall into dust
that which has lived so warmly,
without the muscles rippling
or a nerve trembling,
while even so the soul
inwardly clings fast to everything.
Might I myself fall into dust,
as though I had never lived.

Terrible above all thought
is the dulled night,
into which a spirit can immerse itself
which has only thought,
which has not allowed itself to be guided by Thee,
radiant power of faith!
Alas, what can the Dark One think about
except the dark night?

My songs will live,
long after I have disappeared.
Many a one will tremble before them
who has felt as I do,
whether another has offered them,
or my own hand.
Behold, the songs were allowed to live,
but I disappeared.

My brother, let us look firmly then
upon the Word of God.
Confusion will vanish,
but this will live on for ever.

Do you know how it can arise
in the brain?
If we do not some time, smiling,
behold the word of destruction,

how it hung upon a thread,
which, stretched too tightly,
freed itself from the forehead
laden with flaming blood.
Let us beseech the Grace of God,
let us appeal to His hand,
which lovingly stretched out
the threadlets and the threads.

On the Feast of the Annunciation

The reading for the Feast of the Annunciation, celebrated on 25 March, is St Luke's account (1, 26-38) of the coming of the Angel to Mary, to announce that she will bear the Son of God, and from this well known passage Droste-Hülshoff takes the powerful statement with which her poem begins and which is repeated in the last line of the first strophe: 'for with God nothing shall be impossible.'

As with most of these poems, this is no mere re-telling of a familiar biblical event, though it is redolent with the wonder and significance of it. Rather is it a beautiful evocation of the arrival of spring which speaks also of the stirring on the earth with the coming of the Messiah. Further, it focuses, inevitably, on the figure of the young woman, the chosen one of God, who accepts her overwhelming fate with humility and purity. More still, it expresses in a gentler tone than so many of the poems the sense of the poet herself that she too has been chosen by God and that, with His mercy and guidance, she will come to the faith she so desires.

Needless to say, she expresses this belief without arrogance but in the absolute confidence that nothing is impossible with God, and she links with this confidence that she will find faith the belief that her poetic genius will be allowed to flourish, hence the powerful image of 'bleeding sparks like a stone'.

The reference to Mount Horeb, with the accompanying references to the pillar of fire and the golden calf, is a forceful reminder of the authority of God contained in the Ten Commandments given to Moses. Yet, in complete contrast, Droste-Hülshoff summons up the traditional flower of the Virgin Mary, the modest, simple daisy, to convey the sheer humanity of the young woman as she embraces her great role.

> Yes, His power has no bounds.
> Nothing is impossible with God.
> This shall shine before me like my Northern Star,
> when my sun has set,
> And when on icy blue shores
> I stand in the stark wintertime,
> how shall I survive the remainder of my life?
> Alas, no flame far and wide!
> Yet behold: who signalled to the gentle springtime,
> telling it to embrace the dead earth?
> Yes, His power has no bounds.
> Nothing is impossible with God.
>
> Ah, look, how the hard heart of the earth
> wells up as though with warm tears,
> and how, to nourish its flowers,
> it fills its grey lashes with dew!
> And into the long-dead branches
> there pours a wondrous life,
> and all wait for its guests,
> the joyous throng of leaves.
> How shall I fight against the hope

that has stilled the pleading of my tears
when in truth, the hard heart of the earth
wells up even with warm tears?

Can you pull the millions of leaves
from these dead branches,
and the fresh green of the lava cliffs
from the burnt-out fire?
Why should my heart appear too hard to you,
even though good will burns there
and it would like to unite itself, glowing, with you
all the while it is separating itself, staring, from you.
And, my Almighty Saviour, should not a pale weed
blossom forth from me,
when Thou canst draw the millions of leaves
out of the dead branches?

Ah, if only humility would germinate!
Splendour has dried up.
Once I could easily dream different dreams,
yet that time is like a flash of lightning.
To be sure, I can yearn in remorse;
I can reject my deed;
yet I cannot refresh my tears;
they fall upon the seed and singe it.
And frost and heat must act with one accord,
so that no flower grows from me.
Ah, if only humility would germinate!
Splendour has dried up.

Thus, after all, of all flowers
the daisy is gentle by nature.
First the leaves fall, then the downy bracts,
yet still it goes on blooming tenderly and joyfully.
As soon as the winter storms break
it peeps out in friendly fashion through the snow,
and when spring approaches in pouring rain
it is standing in the cold lake.
Oh, if only I could fall down in faith,
until this little flower reveals itself to me!

To be sure, of all flowers
the daisy is gentle by nature.

Yet like the people once before the gates
round Horeb's sacred mount,
my thoughts flee trembling
when they glimpse this pure sight.
Why do I see only the pillar of fire
and not the mercy of God within it,
so that this steep path where I am
seems immeasurable and like an abyss?
Oh Jesus, only do not let the golden calf
emerge from this wavering,
as it did to the people before the gates. (f)

And if I can bleed no life,
then shall I bleed sparks like a stone!
I know that when they were resting silently
I drove them into slumber,
when I was seeking that which life announced.
Yet, Lord, Thou hast chosen me
that I may stand staring yet firmly founded
like the walls of Thy cliffs.
Thus, in the fire of deeds,
burn me and make me pure,
like the asbestos of the cliff,
and if, then, I can bleed no life,
then I shall bleed sparks like a stone.

(f) *Exodus* 32

On Palm Sunday

It has been suggested (Woesler IV, 2, p.385) that Droste-Hülshoff was unable to join the traditional Palm Sunday procession in 1820 owing to her frequent illnesses (of which there is ample evidence) but watched it from her window. When she speaks, in the penultimate strophe, of the suffering she has endured this year, and which she dedicates to God, she may be referring to her physical ailments or to the confusion and distress caused by her friendship with Heinrich Straube and August von Arnswaldt, or perhaps even to both.

Certainly the poem is based rather on the experience of being the onlooker than on the Gospel reading for the day (*Matthew 21, 1-9*) which tells, quite briefly and without the visual emphasis on the strewing of palms, of Christ's ride into Jerusalem on a donkey. This seems to be a very personal appeal from the young woman, sick physically and racked with guilt and regret, to her Saviour.

> The morning dew is rising.
> So are the palms green?
> Up! Let us go towards Him
> with brightly coloured branches.
> He wishes to come into our house,
> into our rooms.
> Already the pious ones are emerging
> with their song of praise.
>
> I cannot go with you.
> My breath is heavy.
> The arms of the Cross
> are waving from side to side,
> and I can never follow.
> How clear the air is!
> Oh Jesus, sweet radiance!
> Thou comest into my cell,
> into my musty grave.
>
> What shall I offer Thee,
> Thou wondrous, beloved guest?
> I should like to lead Thee
> to a long repose of love.
> Come now, I will adorn Thee,

will bind Thee with flowers,
and Thou shalt not free Thyself,
that I know for sure.

About Thy foot
I will entwine the pure lily
from the right hand of Thy mother
in humble greeting
and so that I may tie Thee up completely
with the garlands of love,
I will entwine about Thy hand
the holy rosary.

I will strew the ground
over and over with palms
to dedicate my suffering to Thee.
That which in this year I have endured ,
often in silence, often more painfully,
lies at Thy feet,
and that must not trouble me:
Thy will is enough for me.

How shall I even so
find my way into the power of Thy love,
so that Thou hast given no thought
at all to my sins!
I will not leave Thee,
even if Thou must depart again at once.
In truth I feel it joyfully:
Thou wilt often come to me again.

On Monday in Holy Week
Of the withered fig-tree

For the Monday in Holy Week, Droste-Hülshoff takes the Gospel reading of St Matthew (21, 18-22) which continues from the Sunday immediately preceding and relates how Jesus, searching for food, came upon a fig-tree by the roadside and, seeing that it had produced only leaves and no fruit to assuage His hunger, cursed it and predicted that it would never produce fruit in future. When it immediately withered, His disciples asked for an explanation, whereupon He used the incident, not as a parable on the nature of the fig-tree itself, and the significance of its withering, but as a lesson on faith: 'Verily I say unto you, if ye have faith and doubt not, ye shall not only do this which is done to the fig tree, but also if ye shall say unto this mountain, Be thou removed and be thou cast into the sea, it shall be done.'

Droste-Hülshoff goes still further in her use of this rather strange little episode, which has taxed theologians, some of whom have seen in it a political message about the state of Israel in the time of Christ and the falseness in some religious observance at that time.

Her poem takes the form of a dialogue between Man, the onlooker, the poet herself, and the fig-tree, and in this way she is able to present two contrasting standpoints, the familiar exposition of her own doubts and questioning, and the pessimistic view of life expressed by the cursed tree, also taken by some critics to be herself. That this is a dialogue is obvious, and it has not seemed necessary to insert the inverted commas used by some editors, but not by Woesler in the *Historisch-Kritische Ausgabe*, and presumably not in any of the manuscripts.

> How dry and barren do you stand there,
> O fig-tree,
> with dry veins empty.
> A wreath of pale leaves
> hangs around you,

rustling like the foam of the sea!
O, man, I must stand here,
must greet you with the greeting of death,
that you seize hold of life,
not leave it.

So how do I cling to life,
O fig-tree,
so that it does not escape me?
O man, free will is the best thing
and wins true loyalty.
If you control pride and doubt
and rein in half-heartedness,
then in these doings
life must remain for you.

Why are you so completely dead,
O fig-tree,
so totally destroyed?
O man, I allowed my life
to take its course on the edge of the earth,
like an abundant dawn.
And alas, I gave no thought to fruit,
and so the Lord God cursed me,
that I might bear witness
to all life.

Who did such a thing to you,
O fig-tree,
through secret betrayal?
O man, the eye of the Lord sees far.
It sees the track of the little worm
in the down on a leaf.
You can hide nothing from it,
nor take anything away from it.
He sees it and knows it.
Already on the first day it lay in the balance.

Surely you died a long time ago,
O fig-tree,
because you are so barren and empty.
O man, the hand of the Lord reaches far

and is so swift and so sure
you hardly see it.
· He takes from you His breath of life,
and you must vanish like mist and smoke.
He has no need of words or time,
and you are gone.

So where is His great mercy,
O fig-tree,
what use is remorse?
O man, think of your guilt,
and think of His faithfulness!
See, in His great mercy,
He placed me here,
that through His wide world
I might call a warning to you
from the depth of my misery.

So is there no hope left in you,
O fig-tree,
no hope in your anguish?
O man, there is no hope in me,
for I am dead, am dead.
O dream of life,
if only I had felt your weight,
if only I had not played so boldly with you,
I would not stand condemned, woe unto me,
annihilated.

On Tuesday in Holy Week
"Thou shalt love thy neighbour"

Droste-Hülshoff bases this poem on the response which Christ gave to His disciples when they asked Him which was the great commandment (*Matthew* 22, 37-41): 'Thou shalt love the Lord thy God with all thy heart, and with all thy soul, and with all thy mind. This is the first and great commandment. And the second is like unto it. Thou shalt love thy neighbour as thyself.' As so often, she faces up to her inadequacy, unable to fulfil this injunction, so simple yet so elusive, and this awareness leads to a confrontation with what she construes as a misspent life. As before in the cycle (See, for example, p.50) and elsewhere on a number of occasions (notably in poems like 'Die rechte Stunde', 'Der Dichter', 'Mein Beruf'), she examines the question of a gift given and received, yet, here, wasted, frittered away like alms to the poor, all too lightly regarded. With this recognition, which torments her for her failure to use her vocation, she see herself approaching the hour of her death, in fear and trepidation, which is yet alleviated at the end of the poem by the belief that God who suffered for her and conquered death will not exact the ultimate price from her.

"Thou shalt love thy neighbour
as thy own soul."
O Lord, how much must still be lacking
before Thy word is fulfilled!
In that case all my thinking must sadden me
with no hope of rescue.
Wherever the eyes may turn,
one sees only foolishness.

My Lord, I must confess that,
no matter if my sins often burn
in deepest chasms,
this one has never tormented me.
Thus to all the flaws
which enflame my breast,
the horror of arrogance
must mortally be added.

And have you abandoned me,
my stern conscience,
because I seemed to hate you
in my fears?
Oh, sharpen your torments,

and allow me to glow
before the eyes of God,
in shreds and covered with bloody marks.

Tell me, did you intend to deceive me?
And can the clinking of coins
which I offered to the poor
defeat your venal word?
Thus, oh gold, oh base gift,
which is meant to achieve everything,
you carry my last hope
to the grave with me.

How often did that which is concealed,
sensuality, press to make its offering
when a countenance quite distorted by wretchedness
filled me with fear,
and did it not soon have to escape
the idle hands,
the hopelessly erring senses,
withered with misery.

O gold, oh base gift,
what little purpose do you serve!
You can only chime the final wafting grace
to the grave.
Thus you have taken love
without compare from me,
so that I can impart it smilingly
to where the children of God can see.

Speak, you senses, you timid ones:
why have you moved away?
Must everything that can delight me
not delight you too?
You have sucked pleasure
in fluttering desire
while anguish vanished
on the day of your rejoicing.

Thus I have squandered
your pounds frivolously,
and for me a penny was enough
for the wound of poverty.
That will still gnaw at me
when body and soul separate,
will fight to battle
with my final fear of death.

I should indeed despair,
for I have committed many crimes,
but since Thou, my God,
hast brought me to this day
when the horror of my soul
has been broken by alien strength,
how should it not trust Him
who broke its bonds?

On Wednesday in Holy Week
Of the Resurrection of the Dead

The reading for the Wednesday in Holy Week is contained in the Gospels of Matthew (22, 23-33), Mark (12,18-27) and Luke (20,27-38), and the context is the response by Jesus to the Sadducees who pose to Him the problem of a man, one of seven brothers, who dies and leaves his wife to the first of his brothers, who then dies and leaves the wife to the next brother, and so on, until she herself dies, after seven marriages. The question they ask is: whose wife is she after her death? Jesus, aware that they are using this issue of worldly status in order to challenge the belief in resurrection, which they are known to reject, addresses that issue with the terse reply: 'Ye do err, not knowing the scriptures, nor the power of God, for in the resurrection they neither marry, nor are given in marriage, but are as the angels of God in heaven.'

However, He then goes on to speak of the much more significant question of resurrection itself, directing them again to the scriptures: '…have ye not read that which was spoken unto you by God, saying I am the God of Abraham, and the God of Isaac, and the God of Jacob? God is not the God of the dead but of the living.' (*Matthew* 22, 29-32)

On this occasion, Droste-Hülshoff does not relate the episode but uses the Gospel reading as her starting-point for a poem which assumes the reality of the Resurrection and examines her thinking on the implications of this reality for the life which she must meanwhile endure.

So, I will go forward, then,
with heavy heart,
since everything will be known to me,
when the dead arise,
and until that time --
this is my greatest anguish --
I must endure all the arrogant questions
that push me towards death,

like a body which, long since unfolded,
through the gentle sap of the plant,
formed with renewed life's energy
into a second body,
how this body can appear again undenied
by the other one
which carried it in his bones
and long since consumed by the third.

That which is many faceted with the soul,
whether of good or bad,
how the most holy power
will dissolve itself in earthly joy,
so that, in those tender hours

when we are as if united with God,
that eternally active enemy
has often found us at our weakest.

And many other things
which I do not need to know
and which push me towards death
– alas, quite insignificant to the pious one!
Yet in my empty heart,
devoid of truth, devoid of repose,
they lie amidst dull pains,
a sharp, steep burden.
Lord, I cannot banish them,
only lock them up firmly and faithfully,
and life rushes by
and Thy day drives them away.
Behold, I can say this truthfully,
but my soul stands firm,
when the day of all days
passes terribly over me.

As if in oppressive sultriness,
a powerful black cloud
becomes more black as it darkens through the night,
so that we plead for cool weather
with all its horrors
and that nameless time
lies like a hot, dark patch
in Thy eternity.

But I shut my eyes tightly
as though with iron chains,
pressed against the cliff
to protect myself from giddiness,
and thus I will go forward
with heavy-laden heart,
and when the dead arise,
all will yet be known to me.

On Maundy Thursday
The washing of the feet

The Gospel reading for Maundy Thursday recounts how, after the Passover feast and knowing that His death was now very close, Jesus washed the feet of His disciples. From this gesture, deeply surprising in itself and questioned above all by Peter, He moved to the significance of it in terms of human relationships: 'Ye call me Master and Lord; and ye say well, for so I am. If I then, your Lord and Master, have washed your feet: ye also ought to wash one another's feet. For I have given you an example, that ye should do as I have done to you. Verily, verily I say unto you; the servant is not greater than his lord; neither he that is sent greater than he that sent him. If ye know these things, happy are ye if ye do them.' (*John* 13, 13-17)

This is a very significant episode and an important message delivered by Christ to those who will so soon be left bereft after His Crucifixion, and Droste-Hülshoff conveys the sense of wonder from the first strophe, with the silence broken only by the sound of breathing from the astonished disciples, and the sound of the water itself as He uses it for this momentous task. She responds to the extraordinary contrast described in the reading between the practical preparations, the filling of the bowl with water and the arrangement about His naked body of the towel with which He dries their feet, and what this whole procedure signifies at this time and in this place.

The poem reflects her emotion as she recognizes what this means in terms of herself and her own life, the responsibility that it places upon her. An important biographical detail contributes to an understanding of her state of mind, if not, perhaps, to a deeper understanding of the poem itself. Some months after she had written it, she revealed in a partially extant letter of late 1821 to Anna von Haxthausen, the relative in whom she confided a great deal, that at this time she was suffering intensely from the headaches which plagued her for much of her life, so much so, she admits, that she was writing under the pressure of the most terrible feelings and feared for her sanity. This would certainly account for the language she uses at the heart of this poem, with the sense of torment and of being tested. The message of Jesus to the disciples reaches her and with it the sense of impending darkness, but the ultimate message with which He leaves them is the far gentler one on which the poem ends, as she embraces the idea that this test is but the prelude to a greater resolution. Presumably it is this hope which is contained in the same letter to her young aunt, when she implies that she has passed through this anguish and is now convinced that she need not fear a recurrence of the overwhelming experience to which the letter and the poem itself bear witness. Our knowledge of her life and much of what she wrote subsequently show that the respite of which she appears to be speaking is a passing one, but in its context, immediately before the poems for Good Friday and Easter Day, the experience itself is most revealing. It is significant, too, that the poem belongs to the very few that Droste-Hülshoff set to music, and one can probably deduce from this that it mattered to her in a particular way.

> O wondrous night, I greet you!
> Lord Jesus washes their feet.
> The air is quite still,
> and one can hear the sound of breathing,
> and the drops falling
> from His holy hand.
>
> When Jesus leans forward,

whole islands bow to this greeting
into the deep sea.
If He has descended so low,
then I must lie for ever
before the feet of my neighbour.

Lord, if as though deranged
my soul is outraged
at all base deeds,
so that I am ready rather
to surrender my life in torment
for Thy glory,
then grant that I may not lament
if Thou hast banished
all shame into my days.
Let my wounds burn
now that Thou hast found me so firm
in such a harsh state.

Oh God, I cannot disguise
how fearful I am in face of those henchmen
whom Thou perhaps hast sent
in sickness or in grief
to deprive me of my senses,
to kill my reason.

It often seems to me
as if Thy stern trial
were about to begin,
as if a cloud were falling like dusk
about the radiance of my spirit,
yet unknown to the masses.

Yet, just as the pains
that enflame my brain are vanishing,
so also does the mist flee,
and, with secret glow,
I feel myself clothed anew
in fresh, strong air.

My Jesus, if I may choose,

I will rather torment myself
with every shame and suffering
than that the splendour of humanity
be taken from me like this,
albeit to my advantage.

Yet if it is so poisoned
that it produces annihilation
when it flows around my heart,
then let me lose it,
that richly endowed spirit,
in order to lead my soul home.
If, then, Thou hast ordained
that I be poured out,
remain a dead stream of water
for the whole of this life,
then shall I go trembling
towards Thy test.

On Good Friday

After her powerful poem for Maundy Thursday, in which she links
the account of the washing of the disciples' feet with her description
of something approaching frenzy in herself as she seeks to
comprehend its message, Droste-Hülshoff again, in this magnificent
poem for Good Friday, places herself close to the scene of the
Crucifixion. She recreates the visual impact so well-known and uses
the details present, to a greater or lesser extent, in all four Gospels,
to evoke the familiar universal drama and, again, seeks to interpret
what it means for her own life, and death.

In these last poems of what is traditionally known as the first part
of the cycle, the young poet seems to be rising to a crescendo in her
craft, responding to the grandeur of the story of Christ's death and
Resurrection in a way which anticipates her achievement in the

future, and particularly in some of her last poems. One may speculate on what lay behind her decision to set the project aside and seek explanations in what we know of what was happening to her on a personal level at this time and in what she writes to those very close to her, and, of course, it is impossible to say for certain whether she intended to resume work on *Das Geistliche Jahr* at some later date. What is apparent is that she has reached a maturity of thought and a command of technique not always present in the poems of the cycle of very few months previously.

Outstanding in this poem is the simplicity, if one can ever use the word to describe her writings, and the absence of complicated imagery. The impact rests in the directness of her description and in her use of features derived from, or sometimes merely implied in, the Gospel accounts with which she has grown up: the baying of the crowd, the instruments of the Crucifixion, the bleeding of the wounds, Christ's cries of anguish and thirst, the gesture of the attendants as they reach up to Him with gall and vinegar. She is faithful to the account particularly in St Matthew, of the events simultaneous with the death of Christ: 'And, behold, the veil of the temple was rent in twain from the top to the bottom; and the earth did quake and the rocks rent'(*Matthew* 27, 51). What is lacking is the appeal to God the Father: 'My God, my God, why hast thou forsaken me?' as reported by Matthew (27, 26) and St John's report of the final words from the Cross 'It is finished' (19, 30). Both are implied, rather, in the single line 'Gänzlich muß den Kelch er trinken' (line 61 'He must drink the chalice to the last drop'), where Droste-Hülshoff uses the word used by Luther to denote the formal cup or chalice in the address of the Son to the Father in the Garden of Gethsemane (*Matthew* 26, 39: 'O my Father, if it be possible, let this cup pass from me: nevertheless not as I will, but as thou wilt').

Droste-Hülshoff, at this point in her life, is not so much

concerned in this poem with the fate of mankind and the fulfilment of a prophecy. For her sense of the significance of the Crucifixion and the death of Christ as the redemption of mankind though love, one must wait twenty-five years, when the great poem 'Gethsemane' (1845/6) pronounces the message of Christianity which, through her grief, she is not yet ready to articulate, or perhaps even to perceive. (See above pp.6-8).

What runs through the present poem is precisely that grief, expressed from its opening lines and reiterated throughout, whether it be in her own tears, or the tears of the little birds, or in the mourning veil assumed by the sun. A questioning tone runs through the poem, too, as indeed it often does in her religious poems, and there is even the ambivalence of her understanding of the cosmic destruction that follows the death of Christ: 'Do they break in joy or pain?' No question remains, however, as she ends her poem in the confidence that this death is for her, for her poor soul, and for the achievement of eternal life for her. By the time she reached 'Gethsemane', within a few months of her own death, her vision had widened and the fulfilment of God's will through the death of His Son, had become a concept which she could embrace on behalf of all mankind.

> Weep, my eyes, weep,
> only rather run over with tears.
> Ah, the day will avail you nothing,
> and the sun will scorn you.
> His eyes are closed,
> the sweet radiance of His eyes.
> Weep, weep, without restraint:
> you can never weep enough.

> When the sun perceived this,

it drew a mourning veil
across its clear eye,
and its tears fall silently.
And I still hope to suck joy
from the world, the bright, lovely world?
Weep, weep my eyes, or rather run over with tears.

Be silent, singing and all the sounds
that delight the heart!
'Crucify him, Crucify him!' roars the crowd,
and the Pharisees laugh.
My Jesus, in the midst of all Thy anguish,
their guilt grieves Thee above all others.
Alas, how did Thy heart feel,
when so many had to fall?

And the poor little birds
are so frightened
that they would rather weep
if their little eyes were not dry.
They sit sadly in the branches,
and no sound rings out anywhere around.
My heart, the poor little birds are silent,
and you must force out your pain.

Away with golden goblets,
sweet wine from a noble stem!
Alas, the hot flame of thirst
still burns Him in His agony,
so that He must cry out aloud in pain,
and heaven and earth must grow pale
as the executioner's lads dare
to reach up to Him with vinegar and gall.

Soft pillows, silken cushions,
can I still long for you,
when my Lord, torn in shreds like this,
must hang upon the hard Cross?
Ah, how have you afflicted Him,
thorn and nail, rod and spear!

Yet, to be sure, the book of guilt lies open,
waiting for His holy blood to close it.

In the earth all the dead
start up as though in horror,
as it begins to grow wet
with the sacred red blood.
They cannot rest any more, those dead ones,
where His precious red blood has flowed.
The ground which has enjoyed such precious drink
Is much too sacred.

He who is Lord in all things
must conquer His own strength
in order that He may struggle with death
and succumb to it.
He must drink the chalice to the last drop.
Oh, man, can you endure it?
His sweet eyes close,
and His heart ceases to beat.

Now that the heart of Jesus is breaking,
the earth breaks in its very depths,
the sea breaks on all its surfaces,
hell breaks in its abysses,
and the hard hearts of the cliffs
break with a loud crash.
Do they break in joy or pain?
Is it the breaking of salvation, or of downfall?

And for whom then has this fight been fought
in these anguished hours,
and the sacred Body been pierced
with the blessed wounds?
Heart, my heart, can you not leap
with the cliffs and the earth
in order only that I be bound anew
to Him in bloody struggle?

Hast Thou given so much, Lord,

for my poor soul?
Is its eternal, everlasting life
so precious to you, for all its guilt and flaws?
In that case, alas, let it not be found
if that would be to sin still more.
Let it not ever see Thy holy wounds with horror.

On Easter Saturday

After the drama of the Crucifixion as conveyed in her poem for
Good Friday, Droste-Hülshoff's emphasis here is on the silence of
the following day. From the first line. this silence is linked with
desolation and emptiness. The silence is not only deep but barren.
The earth is dead, the larks are silent, the sun lacks its dawn: the
world is dull and heavy, rigid and motionless, following the death
of the Son of God, the giver of light and life. There is no Gospel
reading assigned to this day of contemplation, but the link with the
liturgy is present, in the refrain which concludes each strophe. It is
not always the same refrain, though the meaning, the appeal to God
for support, protection, salvation, release, redemption, runs through
the poem and reiterates the message of the Crucifixion. This
traditional response by a congregation gives the poem its link with
the Church and stresses the universality of the significance of the
events it commemorates. At the heart of it, in the middle strophe
of the seven, she focuses for a moment on herself: it is <u>her</u> God who
lies in the grave. However, she immediately rejects this personal
response: her thoughts are as nothing, compared with the impact
on the world as a whole. Eternity replaces the moment, and all
mankind is supported and redeemed by the divine act of salvation.

Deep, barren silence;
the whole earth as if dead!

Larks rise without songs,
the sun without a dawn.
The sky extends itself
across the world, dull and heavy,
rigid and motionless,
like a frozen sea.
Oh, Lord, support us!

The waves of the sea break,
and rage without a sound.
Only the human creatures speak,
yet the echo is eerily silent.
The air around us is
as if turned to stone.
Indeed, no prayer forces its way
through to heaven any more.
Oh, Lord, support us!

Sins have been perpetrated,
too great for any word,
so that the earth must needs vanish
if the Body of Jesus were not holding it inside it.
Still in death His Body full of Grace
supports the world
so that in its guilt
it does not fall to dust.
Oh, Lord, protect us!

Jesus is lying in the grave:
my God lies in His grave.
Yet any thoughts I have are only
mockery compared with that.
Does no Jesus any longer know
the world in all eternity?
No one who forgives,
and no one who sustains?
Oh, Lord, save us!

Ah, to those pious ones
who waited for His salvation,

waited for His mercy,
glory has come
with His sweet presence.
Time past,
the present patience,
the future eternity.
Oh, Lord, redeem us!

Long, long times
look out in faith and trust
through the unknown reaches
towards unknown salvation.
They thought of so many things,
of much blessedness and splendour.
Alas, it was like a game
thought up by children.
Oh, Lord, release us!

Lord, I am speechless
before Thy countenance.
Let all creation crumble;
it cannot bear this day.
Alas, what is approaching with such heavy steps?
Is it eternal night,
is it a sea of sunshine,
in the splendour of a thousand rays?
Oh, Lord, support us!

On Easter Sunday

The grief and then the resignation of the two previous poems give way now to the joy of Easter Day, but the sombre message of the Resurrection cannot be separated from the ineffable mystery of the Crucifixion. This time the individual is present, the representative of all who have seen the wonder of the Death on the Cross and understood its meaning. Joy and sorrow are both there, but the questioning tone of this poem speaks of the mystery which brings the

human being face to face with the recognition that joy cannot exist
without sorrow and that Easter Day reverses the anguish of Good
Friday. As before, the speaker, the poet herself, stands for all
mankind, but, equally, Droste-Hülshoff succeeds in showing herself
isolated in an overwhelming experience which is yet a universal one.

Rejoice, oh world, you have Him back again!
His heaven could not restrain Him.
Oh, rejoice, rejoice, sing songs!
Why are you growing dark, my blessed sight?

It is too much, one can but weep.
Joy stands there like grief.
Who can unite himself with such joy,
when he has seen so much sadness?

I have known unending salvation
through a mystery full of pain,
such as no human mind can hold,
no human heart can feel.

My Lord has risen from the Grave,
and greets all His people there.
And we are free from death and bonds,
And cleansed of the decay of sin.

He has rent His own Body,
to wash us with His Blood.
Who can know this secret
and not melt in the glow of love?

I am supposed to rejoice on this day
with Thy whole Christendom,
and it seems to me that I may dare to do so
when the Unnamed brings me joy.

The blessedness of eternity
has struggled with the agonies of death.
Horror has oppressed eternal perfection
like sinners.

My God, what could move Thee
to this boundless grace?
I cannot stir my thoughts
to contemplate our unmeasured guilt.

Alas, are all the souls of human beings -
priceless commodity though they indeed may be -
are they of so much value, that God must torment Himself
and die in fear and fire?

And are not all the souls of men
in His presence but the breath from lips
and stained with shame and error,
like dreary, dark smoke?

My spirit, do not seek to explain
that which is inexplicable.
The stone of a fall awaits the blind man
when he misses the paths of God.

My Jesus has found them precious
in love and justice.
What more do I wish to know?
His will remains eternally.

Thus may I believe and trust
the splendour of my soul;
thus may I look upwards to heaven
in the image of my God.

I should rejoice on this day;
I do rejoice, my Jesus Christ.
And if I have tears in my eyes,
Thou knowest they are tears of joy.

On Easter Monday
Of the disciples on the way to Emmaus

St Luke relates how two disciples walking on the road from Jerusalem to Emmaus are deep in discussion of the events they have recently experienced. They are joined by a third person who walks with them but whom they do not recognize as Jesus. He asks what they are talking about so earnestly and so sadly. When they tell Him, expressing surprise that He has not heard of the events in Jerusalem, of the Crucifixion of Jesus of Nazareth and of how some of their number had found the tomb empty and guarded by angels who said that He was still alive, though they did not see Him, He challenges their despair and doubt: 'O fools and slow of heart to believe all that the prophets have spoken; ought not Christ to have suffered these things, and to enter into his glory?' (*Luke* 24, 23-24)

He proceeds to expound to them on all the things in the Scriptures relating to Himself. When they reach Emmaus, they persuade Him to join them rather than continuing on His way in the approaching night-time. Only when they prepare to eat together and He breaks the bread do they realize who He is: at this point He vanishes, leaving them to marvel at the encounter: 'Did not our heart burn within us, while he talked with us by the way, and while he opened to us the scriptures?' (24, 32)

It is this aspect of the Gospel story that Droste-Hülshoff seizes upon as the focus of her poem, which begins with the appeal 'Lord, open the scriptures to me' and is concerned, like much of her struggle with her belief, between faith and knowledge. Side by side with faith, however, is the overriding power of love, and with it the transcending emotion of hope. Central to an understanding of the poem are the four lines 'Much is strange to me, / much must seem

dark to me, yet within Thy perfect love / all will be united in joy.'
From this point on she seems to be allying herself with the two
disciples, and with those to whom they relate this strange experience
on their return to Jerusalem: this is the moment of revelation on
which their hope depends now, even if, like them, she knows that
the future will bring more suffering and even the return of despair.
All she can hope for, and what she beseeches God to grant her, is
that this flash of lightning will leave behind His image to guide her.

Lord, open the scriptures to me,
Thy words' loving morning,
so that it may softly touch the heart,
whatever is surely hidden within it.
I myself do not know how to find it,
and yet I am full of hope.
Oh, the clouds will disappear
when the sun is about to shine.

Shall faith be far away,
when love is not lost,
when in nights of silent agony
hope is born again in me?
Thou my God of mercy and loyalty,
who is touched by the wriggling of the little worm,
could it be that Thou hast brought in vain
remorse into this frozen heart?

No, my Lord, Thou hast not done that.
Thy souls are precious to Thee.
Where even just a little spark speaks out,
Thou gladly approacheth with Thy fire.
Oh, I feel indeed how softly
new life is stirring, laying its feeble lips
upon the tender sustenance of Grace.

Much is strange to me,
much must seem dark to me,

yet within Thy perfect love
all will be united in joy.
If the mist was nothing but the evil
which as night-time caused me to despair,
then when my sins disperse
I shall step out of the darkness.

Lord, I thank Thee with my tears
for Thy supremely merciful guidance,
in that in my sinfulness Thou hast
withheld Thy faith from me.
Alas, in my anger, I would
only have glimpsed new sins,
until the voice of conscience
was wafted towards me by the tempest.

Thy mercy is soft and warm
and cannot be devoid of care,
and my heart was too cold and poor
to nourish such a tender guest.
But, as the springs leap up,
torn apart by the agony,
it submerges itself with gentle movements
into the hot red lake.

Lord, I have wept copiously,
so that I often thought
I would perish in the anguish of my soul,
but how has it befallen me today
that I am so full to the brim with joy
and no fear constrains me,
even if the old suffering
still presses hard against my soul?

And thanks to Thy sacred Book
which today is almost open to me,
I can think of not a single curse,
but can only love, can only hope,
can only see Thee leaning forward like a little child,

all loving, all gentle,
and Thy stern words are silent,
and I know not where they are.

But that is only for today.
Ah, it will happen very differently!
For my shame is too great,
and such bliss cannot avail it.
Thou hast only sent Thy flash of lightning
that I might not, mad in my agony,
turn back again towards the glade of idols
that I had abandoned.

Thou unending sweet happiness,
if I must lose Thee again,
only leave behind with me Thy image,
to touch me in my bitterness!
Or, Lord, if from this hour
overwhelming salvation shall arise,
then let the wound of bitterness pass me by,
open, in grief.

CHAPTER SIX

The two parts of the cycle and the cycle as a whole; some critical views

It was at this point, when she had reached what appears as some kind of reconciliation with the doubts which beset her, that Droste-Hülshoff laid aside her work on *Das Geistliche Jahr*. There seems to have been nothing premeditated about the fact that, with the poem for Easter Monday, Droste-Hülshoff suspended her work on the cycle, and there is no evidence, one way or the other, that she intended to continue it at a later date. In the event, of course, almost two decades passed before she completed it.

There are those who attribute her decision not to continue with the project at this point to the response of her mother when she gave her the twenty-five poems with the dedicatory letter, but her own reaction to Therese's response, or rather failure to respond in what looked like a positive way, does not seem to support this view. On the contrary, she writes with understanding when she relates the incident to Anna von Haxthausen, blaming herself for having mistakenly inflicted pain on her mother by what she knows were quite outspoken poems. Although she had acknowledged that they were totally unsuitable for their original purpose, as a gift to her devout step-grandmother, she now seems to see that they must inevitably cause distress to anyone close to her who will be troubled by her conflict with the faith in which she and her nearest and dearest have been brought up.

Others link the abandonment of the project to the emotional turmoil she was suffering as a consequence of the end of her relationship with Heinrich von Straube and her realization that she had been the victim of deliberate collusion among her associates, even some very close to her. The guilt she expresses at her mishandling of the situation is seen as inextricable from a crisis of faith, and thus as a sign that she was no longer in a state of mind to write poems of an essentially spiritual nature which pinpointed her doubts. Again, this does not seem conclusively to have been the case. The questioning tone of many of the poems of the cycle, both the early ones and the late ones, is inherent in this poet, whose manner, throughout her life, was probing, analytical and deeply intellectual.

One cannot absolutely discount either of these theories, and the proper explanation probably combines both of them and adds more. It is really not possible to speak of a spiritual development in the case of Annette von Droste-Hülshoff, or to discern a change in content and approach between what are traditionally called the 1820 poems of the cycle and those of 1839. What there is, however, is a development in poetic skill and in her handling of her material. At all stages of her career, she was conscious of her vocation as a poet and the responsibility this conferred on her, and this may well have been as true in her youth as it was in her maturity. Rather than abandon herself to despair and introspection when this early love affair came to nothing, she appears to have thrown herself into her work, just as, twenty years later, when, following the marriage of Levin Schücking and her acceptance that they had parted for the last time, she found strength and solace in composing her last great poems, which she believed to have been inspired by their love and his belief in her as a poet of considerable substance.

As a young woman barely embarked on her career, with little public recognition as yet, she was certainly filled with ambition and eager to try her hand at a range of projects. The intervening years saw her venturing into many different areas of writing, not always successfully and without consistently completing her sketches. She turned to prose writing, to drama, opera, achieving marked success in the field of the epic, which exploited both her poetic talents and her command of dramatic situations. Her diaries and letters, and those of people close to her, reveal a woman who, for all her dedication to her art, had many other concerns to distract her, not least her love and concern for friends and family. In the background were always her knowledge of and enthusiasm for the natural world, at a time when scientific thought and exploration were assuming new importance. Though not notably politically engaged, she nevertheless displays her knowledge of what was going on in the world about her in this time of great change and uproar. She moved in important circles and was not afraid to exploit her connections and engage in debate in a way which was almost certainly surprising and even shocking in a woman of her background.

All the time, the twenty-five poems lay untouched but, surely, never forgotten, and they came into their own again when, prompted by Christoph Schlüter, she resumed work where she had left off and worked for some time frenziedly on the completion of the project. The plan for this does not seem to have changed, but she was now a mature woman, both personally and artistically, and the project could achieve fruition accordingly.

Although the subject matter and certainly the tone do not change radically between the early poems and the late ones, the technique differs between the two periods, with the later ones showing a much greater sophistication, often characterised by great complexity of language and structure. The thought, too, is more probing and much more analytical: there is no longer the youthful acceptance of some of the early poems. This has now given way to the often tormented contemplation of conflicting thoughts, and the awareness, repeatedly, of an absence of resolution. The artistic maturity of this later part is marked by considerable variety of metre and an abundance of imagery, more striking and original, and often extended over many lines. This is a poet with a firm hold on her art, and the author is a woman who views the many challenges to her beliefs realistically but with no real sense of a conclusion.

One of her most sympathetic and dedicated critics, Cornelius Schröder, whose edition of *Das Geistliche Jahr* (1951) remains a useful source of information and guidance, points out that this is probably as it should be, that even the most 'nearly perfect' Christian can never reach his goal in this world (p.40ff). He returns to her assertion in the dedicatory letter to her mother of 1829, in which she speaks of the work at this point, the first part of *Das Geistliche Jahr*, as being 'wavering in itself, like my mind in its changing moods'. He speaks also of the insight gained through the tormenting experiences of *Das Geistliche Jahr* that a genuinely religious life is 'not rest, but unrest, no certain, steady movement forward, but a weary upward striving, through abysses and over peaks, through dark and light, a perilous walk, which is constantly threatened by the danger of becoming tired, of going astray on paths chosen by oneself, of succumbing to the power of impulses and the seductive magic of the world, that is, to lose sight of the true religious goal.'

For all the somewhat extravagant language, that is a fair

assessment of *Das Geistliche Jahr* and the likely implications of it for Droste-Hülshoff herself and its effect on the attentive reader. More succinctly, but no less effectively, a much more recent critic, John Guthrie, asserts: 'The hallmark of her feeling is the heartfelt, fervent tone which dominates the cycle', but this remark, which is hardly to be contradicted, is embedded in a more complicated assessment by Guthrie of the work which leads into the quite problematic issue of the ambivalent evaluations of *Das Geistliche Jahr*. What Guthrie says, again uncontentiously, is this: 'In her poetry, reason and feeling are no longer in unison. Reason, the backbone of the Enlightenment, does not give her the answers she desires. It conflicts with feeling; it is a curse......This dichotomy lends the poetry tension' (p. 106).

However, this tension is already inherent in the very concept of the cycle, and commentators have engaged through the decades in debate about its nature and intention. Is it a *confession*, a traditional statement of belief (Guthrie p.104)? Is it, as some have maintained more deprecatingly, no more than a collection of verses for a hymn book (*Gesangbuchverse*)? Even Droste-Hülshoff's most positive critics have struggled to assess it and to give it its place within her whole *œuvre,* with the eminent Friedrich Gundolf dismissing the poems of the cycle as 'not belonging as art to the greatest of Annette's works', though this in an essay which raises her to the level of a secular saint both as a woman and a poet (p.193). It is important, too, that this often quoted assessment is followed by a massive concession, when Gundolf continues: 'as a human testimony they are to be cherished and wondered at, precisely through the struggle between Eros and Agape in terms of their feeling, between unfettered expression and pious calm in their tone.... They are the hoarse prayers of a desperate woman who is forcing herself to become a guardian of souls.' These evaluations which, incidentally, do not benefit from translation, belong to a much earlier generation, of course, but they serve to demonstrate something of the difficulty of viewing the work as a whole today. The difficulty arises not least from whether one regards the work primarily as a religious document, or as a piece of literature, whereas it is actually a fusion of the two, and uniquely attempting to be both at the same time.

In concluding this necessarily brief account of scholarly assessments of this puzzling work, one may cite the statements by Emil Staiger (p.50): '*Das Geistliche Jahr* lies before us uncompleted in the broadest sense of the word' and by Clemens Heselhaus who, perhaps more than anyone, has shown the depth of his understanding of her achievement: '*Das Geistliche Jahr* is a genuine work of poetry, magnificent, shattering in its brittle obscurity, and its enormous burden of thought' (1950, p.98). It is almost certainly a mistake to attempt to place this work in any category, or to assign to it a ranking within Droste-Hülshoff's *œuvre*. Rather one should see it as a part – an important part – of her whole work and being, just one key to a doorway secured many times over. After that lengthy digression, one may move to the second, longer part of *Das Geistliche Jahr*, just as she herself took it up again after the greater part of her adult life.

CHAPTER SEVEN

1839 poems

On the first Sunday after Easter
Jesus passes through closed doors and says:
'Peace be unto you'

For this first poem of the later part of *Das Geistliche Jahr* Droste-Hülshoff uses the powerful passage from St John, when he describes the appearance of Jesus to Mary Magdalene at the empty tomb and, after that to the disciples assembled behind closed doors, where they have taken refuge out of fear of the Jews. Two quotations from the Gospel dominate the encounters: Christ's address to Mary by name, when she has failed to recognize Him, and His commendation to the disciples 'Peace be unto you' (*John* 20 19-31), but Droste-Hülshoff takes these as if directed at herself in this poem which speaks of her own faith, or lack of it. She is the child, excluded and in grief, deprived of peace and salvation, of companionship and of what she sees as her inheritance, the seeds of faith waiting for the nurturing power of the sun.

The image of the closed door is transferred to her own being as she waits for Him to enter, the merciful Lord in whom, despite her confusion and seeming lack of faith, she does most fervently trust. This is, of course, an intensely personal poem, and, as she embarks on the second phase of the cycle, one may well ask what has happened in the intervening years to the faith that she so earnestly seeks. Always, still, there is the questioning tone, the desperate seeking, and yet, in this intimate declaration of a closeness with her Saviour, one senses already the answer, and this despite the familiar self-accusations, the implied comparison of herself with the sinner, the publican, the lost lamb.

> And if Thou hast given Thy peace
> to all who crave Thy salvation,
> then I shall also raise my voice:
> here I am, Father, give me my portion, too.
> Why should I, a child shut out,
> pining alone, weep for my inheritance?
> Why should Thy sun not shine
> where there are good seeds in the ground?
>
> Often I believe that all right to prayer
> has been taken from me, when it is so sad and lukewarm.
> Only patient waiting can avail me,
> and a fixed gaze up towards the blue of the sky.
> Yet, Lord, thou who hast befriended the publican,
> do not permit me to drown in night;
> Thy voice calls indeed to the lost lamb,
> and Thou hast come into the world for the sake of the sinner.
>
> I know full well how things stand within my soul,
> how bereft of faith, how defiant and confused,
> so that, alas, much must remain concealed.
> I feel how it buzzes through my nerves,
> and feebly I follow its wretched track.
> My helper, Thou knowest well
> that which I cannot fathom and knowest well how to find it.
> Thou art the physician; I am but the patient.
>
> And if Thou hast gazed deeply into my sins,
> as no human eye can see,

then Thou hast seen how in the deepest chasms
many a dark and heavy illusion slumbers still.
Yet I know, too, that no tear slips away
that Thy faithful hand has not weighed up,
and that no sigh has escaped this breast
that has not reached Thy merciful ear.

Thou who canst pass through closed doors,
behold: my breast is a closed gate.
I am too weak to move the bolts
and yet Thou seest how tremulously I stand before it.
Break in, break in! Ah, enter with Thy might!
Lend me the strength that Thou hast taken from me.
Ah, let me see the archway of Thy peace!
And may Thy sun shine into my night!

I shall not move 'til I have seen a ray of light,
even if it be faint as the glimmer of a worm.
And I will not go from this threshold
'til I have heard the breath from Thy voice.
And so, my Father, speak; speak also to me
with that voice that called the name of Mary
when weeping she turned away and did not recognize Thee.
Oh, say "My child, peace be with you".

On the Second Sunday after Easter
The Good Shepherd, *John* 10, 11-16

Although the declared text that forms the basis of this poem is the
well-known passage from St John about the good shepherd and his
care for his sheep, Droste-Hülshoff again uses this in a wide-ranging
and deeply personal way to speak of her own sinfulness, the
wretched lamb trusting in the Shepherd for salvation. The lost
lamb of the preceding poem is here again, but the context is very
different, for the gentle voice has been replaced by a new
forcefulness.

A new element enters the cycle with the tone of exhortation that runs through it, and the accusations directed at those with authority and power, and, perhaps above all, the use of the mark of Cain to represent guilt. The sermonizing tone gives way only at the last to the plea for redemption, expressed in the appeal for that mark to be washed away with tears.

A good shepherd never leaves his sheep!
Alas, shepherd, to whom a wretched lamb
will one day call in lamentation, whimpering with fear!
A wounded, bleeding creature, jumbled and covered in sludge.
What do you want to say? Be silent!
Your word is dead, like the mark on the forehead of Cain.

Woe to you, princes, you who weigh up
the souls of the people against profit and earthly growth!
Woe to you parents, to whom the shining failings of the child
are dearer far than simplicity lacking brightness.
You have striven after judgment. Speak not of honour; they
Do not know your honour on the other side.

Woe to you, heads of families, who have assumed
the role of servant only like a hired hand.
You are unworthy to be chosen as a shepherd,
you friendless man, you foolish woman.
Did you know and yet say nothing?
Behold, a mark burns on the hand of each of you.

And woe, woe to them all, into whose hands
was entrusted abundant wealth!
Woe, you teachers, who have poisoned
with scorn and arrogance hearts easy to direct.
Coins stretched out in front of you,
you have not buried them deep, but have stained them with rust.

Yet, are you free? Can you then pronounce so boldly
the words of banishment over a thousand people?
If someone is lacking crown and authority, house and court,

does duty exclude him from their bounds?
Just think! It is a difficult question and it concerns
your soul and the souls of strangers. Just think about it!

Whenever the ear of a child hangs on your lips,
whenever the gaze of a child reads in your eyes,
whenever every bold word that pushes forward
flows into tender ears like hot lead,
are you not then the shepherd?
Is it not your fault if the poor lamb goes astray?

And when an immature spirit, a blunt mind,
listens inquisitively to every word from you,
wishes to gain agreement about everything,
eagerly sketches every gesture,
ah! does not that face say:
"I pay heed to you, by God, do not lead me astray!"

If, Lord, on this day Thou hast revealed to me
that which I never before so earnestly contemplated,
then do I kneel before Thee, pouring myself out in pleas.
Here is the will: now give me the strength!
That mind so rash and foolish:
place Thy firm hand upon it, until it slips away.

Thou canst restrain the thunder with Thy breath,
draw forth islands of palms from the parched sand:
oh, help me, too, to dam the raging river.
Let not the mark of Cain burn on my forehead,
and, if perchance it is there, Lord,
take Thou my tears and wash it hence.

On the Third Sunday after Easter
"A little while and you will see me."

The words of Christ as reported by St John receive their rebuttal
in the stark opening statement of this poem, in which not seeing

Him is symbolic of the lack of faith Droste-Hülshoff expresses, in all the torment she suffers as a consequence. The tender, consoling context is absent, and if one looks at the words of Jesus to His disciples one can see, in contrast, the despair which she feels. Jesus senses their confusion and gives them words of hope and succour in their bereavement: 'Do you inquire among yourselves of that I said, A little while and ye shall not see me, and again, a little while and ye shall see me? Verily, verily, I say unto you, that ye shall weep and lament, but the world shall rejoice: and ye shall be sorrowful, but your sorrow shall be turned into joy.' (John 16, 19-20) Not for Droste-Hülshoff, at least not at first in the poem, is the promise of joy coming from sorrow, but the familiar inner turmoil which so often forbids the realization of the faith she dimly perceives and so fervently desires.

However, as this great poem reaches its climax with the powerful visual images of natural phenomena, and the storm subsides, the mist clears to reveal the promised joy. Then the context of Christ's message of hope, not uttered in the poem but doubtless familiar to Droste-Hülshoff and those to whom she addresses herself, becomes clear. Not for nothing has this been described by one of her foremost interpreters as 'the most unforgettable of all her poems' (Emil Staiger, p.44), and it signals the distance she has come, emotionally but more importantly artistically, in the intervening years.

Yet even so, a poem which reaches a peak of spiritual recognition contains in its central strophe the striking acknowledgement that knowledge has killed belief and that only what she has read in books occurs to her now, when what she needs is faith. This bitter thought passes, however, to give way to joy, as empty wisdom falls away and with the tears of the prophet comes the breath of grace to reveal the God she seeks and now at last has found.

CHAPTER SEVEN

I cannot see Thee.
Where art Thou, then, my treasure, my breath of life?
Canst Thou not blow, so that my ear can hear it?
Why dost Thou seem like mist, why dost Thou flutter around
like smoke, when my eye turns towards Thy signs?
My light in the desert,
my Aaron's rod which could gently bring forth leaves,
you do not do it.
Thus I must atone for my own guilt, and my own foolishness.

The day is hot,
the sun blazes forth from the wall of my cell.
A trusting little bird flutters in and out,
its glistening eye asks me unflinchingly:
"Does the Lord not look out of these windows?"
What are you asking?
I must needs lower my head and blush.
Oh, bitter shame!
My knowledge had to kill my faith.

The cloud climbs up,
and slowly a sulphurous cloak
has covered the azure structure.
The breezes waft so warm and full of sighs,
and groans of fear stir in the branches.
The herd coughs.
What does the dumb animal sense? Is it the warmth of your body?
I stand with my head bowed.
My Lord, touch me, so that I may feel Thee!

A clap of thunder!
Horror has seized hold of the stricken forest.
I see my bird cowering in its nest, how branch rubs
groaning and cracking against branch, how streak after streak
of lightning jerks through the lanes of sulphur.
I follow it with my gaze.
Is it not Thy light, mighty Being?
Why then, alas,
why does nothing come to me but what I have read?

The darkness yields,
and, like soft weeping, the dew
falls from the clouds; whispering far and near.
The sun lowers its golden staff of mercy,
and suddenly the arc of peace stands there.
But what is this? Does my eye become moist?
Is not the rain a product of the mist?
I feel so light.
How is it? Can then the rubbing of the stalk touch me?

On mountain peaks
a prophet stood and looked for Thee, as I do.
Then did a storm break the branch of the giant pine,
and fire consume its way through the tree-tops.
Yet the visitor from the wilderness stood unshaken.
But then there came a breeze
like the breath of grace, and trembling and defeated
the prophet sank to his knees
and wept aloud, and he had found Thee.

So has Thy breath proclaimed to me
that which was hidden in the storm
and did not solve itself in the lightning?
Then I will also wait: my coffin is already growing.
The rain is falling on my place of slumber.
Then will the misty schemes of empty wisdom
vanish like smoke,
and I shall also see,
and no-one will take away my joy from me.

On the Fourth Sunday after Easter
"I am going to Him who has sent me", *John* 16, 5-14

As the basis for this poem Droste-Hülshoff takes the reading from
St John in which Jesus tells His disciples just before His Crucifixion
that He is going away and that for a while they will not see Him.

Knowing that they are puzzled by His words but reluctant to ask for an explanation, He goes further: 'I came forth from the Father and am come into the world: again I leave the world and go to the Father.' With the disciples more satisfied with His less enigmatic prediction, He moves to the great assurance: 'In the world ye shall have tribulation but be of good cheer: I have overcome the world.'

This poem, like that for the Sixth Sunday after Easter, shows Droste-Hülshoff placing herself within the context of a time which she saw as threatening the old order, something she expresses most explicitly in her poem for Ascension Day: 'I have been born in a time of trial./ After a long period of tranquillity in faith,/ crimes which had vanished have now renewed themselves.' (See p.131- 132) It is as though her personal guilt, so much the keynote of the cycle, leads her to take responsibility for the age in which she lives, and to appoint herself as a spokesman against it. This is not a lasting stance, however, and, though this group of poems may be seen in such a light, she reverts to the more familiar role of the bearer of a personal guilt.

I shall not pass before Thy people,
a noble flame of grace.
No: I must stand like Sodom's pillar,
a heavy life turned to stone,
and around me I must see
as in a dream the wanderers swaying past.

And even if a wasteland surrounds me
and the mist almost suffocates me,
and a sandstorm clouds my eyes,
I know that my heart holds fast to Thee,
loves Thee,
and that Thou hast sent me.

From Thee I have my breath of life;
Thou hast made me immortal.
No heat, no dryness harms me.
I know that I am in Thy care,
even if I must stand here
like a prophet of the night.

I raise up my voice,
a herald of the desert in the face of peril.
Wake up, you dreamers, look up!
The dawn is in the sky:
only look up!
Only not backwards, for there stands death.

Only look upwards, only not backwards!
Leave human wisdom behind you,
for that is death, its empty happiness
is like a painted grave.
Oh, lift your eyes!
The sky is so gentle and so rich.

If only I could lift my eyes,
my stony eyes, towards the blueness:
how might I, sick with love,
suck from the firmament the gentle dew.
Yet nature
and guilt have closed my eyes.

Will the crust never lift?
Ah, one day, one day it must happen.
When Sodom's pillar comes to life,
my hour will also come,
when a shudder will pass through
the poor bloodless stone.

Then shall I know what I am
and why I am so weak and rigid with death.
Then shall I know what has driven
my clear senses towards that wasteland.
Then shall I kneel down
before Him who has sent me.

On the Fifth Sunday after Easter

"Thou shalt ask in my name, and thou shalt receive."
"Now do we know that Thou knowest everything."

This is a beautiful poem, typical of Droste-Hülshoff at her mature best, and it stands alongside those great poems of more obviously secular content which mark the closing phases of her creative life. The exchange between Christ and His disciples immediately before His arrest and Crucifixion continues from the preceding poem, and this one has as its heading her rendering of the words of the Gospel. St John reports the relevant parts of the conversation thus, with the words of Jesus: 'Verily, verily, I say unto you, Whatsoever ye shall ask the Father in my name he will give it you.'(16, 23) and the response of the disciples: 'Now are we sure that thou knowest all things, and needest not that any man should ask thee; by this we believe that thou camest forth from God.' Jesus answered them: 'Do ye now believe? Behold the hour cometh, yea is now come, that ye shall be scattered, every man to his own, and shall leave me alone; and yet I am not alone, because the Father is with me.' (16, 30-32)

On the basis of this great statement of faith and of belief in the consoling power of God the Father, Droste-Hülshoff reveals herself as the suppliant, the loving child, the handmaid, in a poem which contains rare touches of autobiographical detail. This is the mature poet, frail and sick, aware as ever of her vocation, yet declaring, again as elsewhere, her indifference to worldly fame. Within a small group of poems which refer to the state of upheaval in the Church at this time and her sense of guilt at being unwittingly a part of it (See above, p.125), this poem stands out as a profound expression of her sense of herself as a lone voice which speaks, not above the tumult of events which threaten society, but as a humble individual standing before her Creator. It links the familiar Gospel reading with a very personal statement of her own spiritual state in a cycle which is far from being a mere collection of poems relating to the Church year and much more a reflection of the spiritual life of one individual.

I may pray in His name,
this He has told me Himself.
The handmaiden may step before her Creator
with His temple of grace.
Oh, sweet right given unto me!
Oh, trust which sprouts forth from Him.
How do I know today of no trembling
when His sunshine flows about me!

Thus, my Creator, in the name of Jesus
do I step before Thy countenance.
Where the blind stand, and the lame,
there is my place and my judgment.
And if I am one of the lowliest
who kneel beneath His shield,
Thy over-abundant hand is filled
for all, for everyone.

Trusting, I will approach Thee,
and even if my lips were to speak foolishness,
I will receive nothing but mercy.
Thou shalt give to me that which is wholesome.
Even if my thoughts are feeble and misguided,
I shall bring them to Thee trustingly,
and Thou shalt decide the boundaries Thyself,
and faithfully receive that which is best in me.

I ask not for earthly happiness,
only now and then for a ray of light
that Thy hands become visible,
that I can sense Thy love,

only in the troubles of life
for resignation's merciful greeting:
then Thou shalt already know best
how much I can endure and must endure.

Nor will I ask Thee for fame
for which my shoulders are much too weak.
Let my consciousness be awake
only in the midst of human voices, so that,
however opinions may move around and run their course,
nevertheless there is One who never errs,
and every word which knows Him not
will grieve me a thousand times over.

Health, precious earthly fiefdom,
alas, I have lacked thee painfully.
Yet I can only beg for this:
that my soul should remain undisturbed,
that the feeble mist may not press upon
my whirling thoughts;
that through the barriers of the most frightening fog
I may always discern Thy day.

I am not short of the love of friends:
everyone is good to the one who suffers.
If my impulses grow stronger or grow fewer,
I place all this in Thy care.
Oh, protect me from that gentleness
which is much too silent in the face of my faults.
Hold Thou the mirror before my face
when the right hand of a friend is hesitant.

I should like to ask for much more,
but it is better that I kneel in silence here.
He who suffered for me on the Cross,
my gentle advocate, is standing by my side.
I wander always in darkness.
It was always He who cast the rays of light.
He who knows everything, should He not know
what his poor handmaid needs?

On Ascension Day

The final verses of St Mark's Gospel relate how Jesus appeared to the disciples and gave them His last words of instruction, that they should go out into the world and preach, and how He was then taken up into heaven, to sit at the right hand of God. Droste-Hülshoff uses this momentous event to express her own desire to love and serve God also. She unites herself with those other servants of Christ, and in particular, she singles out Martha, another woman who served in the most humble way, according to the Gospel, and whom she would gladly emulate.

At this point she introduces a contemporary reference, to the discord in the Church in her time. She is almost certainly thinking in particular of the arguments raging in her own homeland of Westphalia during her own lifetime. The events of 1837-38 culminated in the so-called 'Kölner Kirchenstreit', which was focused on the question of the religion of children of mixed faith marriages, a conflict, therefore, between Church and State. (See Woesler IV, 2, p.220.) That Droste-Hülshoff was deeply concerned at the ensuing events and even violence emerges in a series of letters to her mother during February 1838, in which she ranges characteristically from trivial domestic matters to the momentous circumstances which lead her to speak, in the fifth strophe of this poem, of a resurgence in disturbances thought buried during 'a long period of tranquillity'. This leads to the question which, directly related to her own time and place, can be seen to run through all her considerations of her faith, for love, so central to it, cannot be separated from suffering, whether of the individual, herself even, or of Christ on the Cross.

Droste-Hülshoff was, indeed, born in a time of trial, but this she sees as no negative feature of her faith but as a strengthening force, with suffering contributing to the power of her belief, and of belief in general. Thus the penultimate strophe is one of her rare statements of optimism, not about herself - though that is undoubtedly the implication - but rather about the possibility that faith can flourish through adversity, and gain in strength. It is also a rare poem in that it links the woman to her age.

He belonged to her for thirty three years.
The time has passed, has gone!
How bare of all brightness is she now,
that barren earth upon which I exist and breathe!
How might I not live, when His breath
sweetened the air, when His pure eye
has blessed each plant and every stone?
Why not me? Why only not me?
Oh, Lord, Thou mightest have blessed me too,

I would have crept after Thee everywhere
and would have secretly observed
my beloved Lord, from afar,
hidden by the green embankment of bushes.
I would have turned to Martha,
asking for a small task for my hand to perform,
perhaps to make the fire for Thy meal,
to go to the well, to air the room for Thee.
Thou wouldst have recognized my love indeed.

And outside, in the dense crowd of the people,
I would have concealed myself and listened,
and so willingly have exchanged all other pleasures
for Thy words, warm and full of life.
I would have wished to kneel with Mary Magdalene,
and my tear, too, would have had to gleam
upon Thy foot, and then perhaps, - ah just perhaps!-
Thy blessed words would really have come to me:
"Go hence, your sins are forgiven you also."

In vain! And almost two thousand years
have now approached their close,
since the earth last cradled
her sweet Guest in Bethany.
Already for a long time Thy martyrs have been elevated,
and the foe has long sown weeds;
the kingdom of Thy church has long been split,
and the bow laden with toil hangs grieving
on Thy tree, and yet the root remains.

I have been born in a time of trial.
After a long period of tranquillity in faith,
crimes which had vanished have now renewed themselves.
We bear again burdens almost forgotten
and once more Thy sacrifices have been consecrated.
Ah, is not love more blessed in suffering?
Art Thou not closer when grief weeps,
when three are gathered in Thy name,
than thousands adorned and in the clothes of feast days?

It can be seen how the rich flame of faith
waves above in the storm,
how many a one who previously was like a sleepwalker
now moves his limbs renewed and strong.
The sick are made well, and he who lay
and dreamt has been awoken by the striking of the hour.
That which before was fluttering, scattered in the world,
has placed itself around Thy banner,
and every ancient, unbending dawn has broken.

What more do I want? Is it granted to the servant
to master the gift of his lord?
Whatever you do, let it be acceptable to Him.
And even if Thy love is a flaming star,
if Thou wishest to cleanse Thy possessions through fire,
like asbestos, from the plague of rotten places,
we shall see Thy hand and be consoled.
No matter if the flaming pillar rages over us,
we shall see Thy hand and stand firm.

On the Sixth Sunday after Easter
(also: On the Sunday before Whitsun)

This is one of the most puzzling poems of the cycle, and it seems to have puzzled Droste-Hülshoff herself. In a letter to Wilhelm Junkmann, one of her most intellectually informed and objective confidants, she writes almost as though it has arisen without her participation. The word she uses to describe it is 'demagogisch': it has become quite demagogic without her willing it that way. Her uncle, with whom she is staying at the time, calls it 'a spiritual march' ('einen geistlichen Marsch'). It seems clear that she is referring to the original lines which she subsequently replaced with the strophe which stands as the fourth in the editions. What she originally wrote can be rendered as follows:

> And each one stands at his post,
> And it is our duty to stay standing
> No matter how it blows and rages above us.
> We do not sway. We do not falter.
> Whosoever does not break here will not break in the future.

This translation supplies some punctuation where none exists in her original version, but the meaning is clear even without it: this is a statement of resolution in the face of a possibly destructive fate.

The question remains why she believed this constituted a demagogic, perhaps even hypocritical, stance, and why she told Junkmann that it demonstrated how it was possible to misinterpret the Bible (Letter dated 26 August 1839). The Gospel reading (*John*, 15, 26 – 16, 4) culminates in the prophecy of Christ to His disciples, warning them to be prepared for future persecution: 'They shall put you out of the synagogues: yea, the time cometh that whosoever killeth you will think that he doeth God service. And these things will they do unto you, because they have not known the Father, nor me. But these things have I told you, that when the time shall come, ye may remember that I told you of them. And these things I told you not at the beginning, because I was with you.'

One may ponder on the spiritual content, but it remains that the poem reflects Droste-Hülshoff's command of the dramatic moment, a feature so vividly present in the epic poems at which in the intervening years she had excelled. The brilliant evocation of the soldiers watching in the stormy night, the anticipation of the moment of their awakening by the sound of the bell, the call to duty: all these details could come straight out of one of those ballads or epic poems which show her so deeply aware of the human being in a powerfully moving situation which threatens to change his life

> Wake up! The clock has moved
> towards the minute.
> A new wheel has gently joined up
> with the rusty workings.
> The spring rises up; the hammer falls.
>
> Just as the guard startles the soldiers on the watch
> out of their dull rest,
> thus does the sound of the bell call to us
> through the sultry, stormy night.
> What is your name? Who are you then?
>
> And many a man who in his long dream
> almost slept through his own name
> now pushed his wretched quilt aside
> and quickly called out the password,
> just as the bell was speaking in deep and sombre tones.
>
> Who in such a time might wish
> to exclude himself from Thy army?

That which spring and sunshine has scattered
searches indeed for its home in the storm.
Only vagabonds remain outside.

To the least one was given his important portion;
no man has his place to no avail.
May that which is elevated shine upon us
from the edge of the battlements to give us strength and salvation.
Yet only the mass protects the land.

Even if Thy hand has assigned me
only to a humble post,
nevertheless the breath of the word
that wanders fearless through the world came to me,
whether it be dark or light.

Let each one only do what he can
in order that his hand should stand spear against spear.
Let the humble man join in loyally,
and the exalted man demonstrate his strength.
Then shall I know indeed who will bring salvation.

On Whit Sunday

"Peace I leave with you, my peace I give unto you: not as the world
giveth give I unto you. Let not your heart be troubled, neither let
it be afraid. Ye have heard how I said unto you, I go away and come
again unto you. If ye loved me ye would rejoice, because I said, I go
unto the Father, for my Father is greater than I." (*John* 14, 27-28)

St John relates how Jesus promised that the Holy Spirit would
come, and how He left His disciples with this great assurance that
they would not be left comfortless when He had departed. The
words of this great promise lie at the heart of this beautiful poem
and yet they are not reiterated by Droste-Hülshoff, who

concentrates instead on the crowd, not individuals but men and women, old and young, representing all those who wait for this great moment, future generations perhaps, not tied to a particular time or place. Nor is she herself present, as she so often is in the poems of the cycle, for this is a universal statement of a great truth.

This very powerful poem is an important example of the way in which Droste-Hülshoff's poems, especially those of her later career, overlap in their impact. Though clearly occupying a central place in *Das Geistliche Jahr*, this poem for Whit Sunday is strikingly reminiscent of her great ballads, in evocation of drama and atmosphere: one thinks, for example, of 'Der Fundator' or 'Der Knabe im Moor', but one could cite many more, most of them stemming from this period of her creative life. Significant, also, is her use here of questions, to convey both the tension of the moment, and the sheer wonder of this momentous event. As in her finest nature poems, too, the poem achieves its impact not only with the visual descriptions but also, and perhaps even more effectively, with her use of a variety of sounds, which break through the silence of the day stated so simply in the first line, and the silence of the waiting crowd.

Wilhelm Gössmann (pp.160-187) devotes a whole section to a detailed analysis of this poem, emphasising the visual quality and the way in which Droste-Hülshoff creates a powerful sense of time and place.

> The day was still. The sun stood so clear
> against the unsullied vaulting.
> The air, as though parched in the fire of the Orient,
> let its wings drop dully.
> Look, a little crowd of people, men, old men too,
> and women kneeling. No words resound.
> They are praying softly.

Where is the Comforter, the faithful sanctuary,
whom as Thou hast gone away,
Thou hast promised to Thy people?
They do not despair: Thy word stands firm,
and yet this time must surely seem frightening and bleak.
The hours are creeping past. Already they have been waiting
for forty days and nights in silent weeping, watching for Thee.

Where is He? Where? Hour upon hour,
one minute follows another.
Where can He be? And if the lips are silent,
the soul is asking it and quietly bleeding.
The whirlwind stirs up dust, the tiger groans
and lumbers spluttering through the billowing sand.
The snake thirsts. (f)

Then, hear, a gentle murmuring sound arises. It becomes
louder and louder, until it sounds like the roaring of a tempest.
The blades of grass stand unbowed.
The palm tree, stiff, astonished, seems to be listening.
What is that trembling through the pious crowd?
What is causing them to exchange fearful, glowing glances?
Look up! Behold!

It is He, it's He! The flame leaps up
above each head. What wondrous circling,
welling up and jerking through the veins!
The future breaks. The sluice gates open,
and the Word streams forth unhampered,
now the cry of the herald
and now as a gentle, pleading whisper.

Oh, light, oh Comforter! art Thou proclaimed
only to that time, only to that crowd?
Not to us, not everywhere,
where a single soul finds itself sleepless and devoid of comfort.
I thirst in the heavy night.
Oh shine, before my eyes grow completely blind.
They weep and are awake.

(f) Here she has the alternative 'his jaws', presumably referring to the tiger, an instance where her second, and sometimes third and fourth, thoughts were indeed new thoughts, and not simply verbal variations.

On Whit Monday

The Gospel reference is St John's report of the powerful words of Christ which speak of the need for faith: 'For God so loved the world that He gave His only begotten Son that whosoever believeth in Him should not perish but have everlasting life' (John 3, 16), but Droste-Hülshoff concentrates not on these words of succour but, obsessed as so often with her bleak belief in her inability to experience faith, moves to His later warning: '..but he that believeth not is condemned already' (v.18), even going so far as to equate condemnation explicitly with death. Yet out of that seemingly hopeless position emerges this great statement of the power of Love, made manifest in the gift of God to the world and His sowing thereby of the seed of love in the human heart. It is upon that belief that the poem rises to a hymn of praise of Love itself, and of the nature of a loving God. The teaching of her Church, moreover, leads her to the confidence that the mere desire for faith is a sacrament in itself, and the poem represents a high point in her search, a mellow statement, at the end of her life, that the elusive goal may yet be achieved.

If it is faith alone that Thou hast promised,
Then I am dead.
Oh, faith, I have need of it,
like the coursing of living blood!
But I do not have it
Ah, if in place of faith Thou wilt not accept love,
and the tear-laden tribute of yearning,
then I do not know how I may still have hope.
The staff is broken, the measure is full
in judgment of me.

My Saviour, who loves as no one loves,
dost Thou feel no compassion
when someone made in Thy image
kneels, dying of fear, so sick and devastated,
on cold stone and pleads with Thee?
Is Thy divine breath only faith, then?
Hast Thou not also
with Thine own blood
sown love deep in our breast?
Oh, please be gentle!

Thou hast pronounced a harsh and heavy word:
that "he who does not believe is judged".
In that case I am broken totally.
Yet He who gave His Son, the only begotten One,
for sinners and for pious ones alike,
will not leave me so deprived.
I, poorest of the lost ones, look to Him
for but one word of hope:
He is so rich,
my light of Grace.

Thou gentle One, who so graciously
Thyself hast sealed the baptism of desire
with the honour of a sacrament,
I do not doubt
that Thou hast surely also blessed
the longing for faith, the sanctity of yearning.
Otherwise Thou wouldst in truth not be
so great in kindness and so full of faithfulness,
if Thou wouldst break a little branch
out of which the flower is bursting and has promised fruit.

Whatever wrong I may have committed
through the errors of my reason,
I have surely atoned for it for many a day and many weeks.
So be Thou close to me!
I will hope and yearn and endure

according to the strength which I know I have bent
by my own guilt and cannot set to rights again.
Then, faithful One,
Thou wilt indeed grant faith
which brings forth aid.

On the First Sunday after Whitsun (Trinity Sunday)

The instructions which Christ gives to His disciples, as recorded at
the close of St Matthew's account, that they should go out and preach
to the peoples and baptize them (*Matthew* 18, 18-20) end with the
promise 'and lo, I am with you always, even unto the end of the world'.
It is these instructions, and this promise which Droste-Hülshoff takes
up for this very personal poem, which speaks of her own baptism as
an infant, of how the sign of the Cross accompanies her through her
life and of her commitment to Christ above all others. Although she
is able, here as so often, to see the limitations of reason, and the
absence of clarity in the human word, the Cross, made on her
forehead at the time of her baptism, is a source of confidence and
enlightenment. When, in the third strophe, she admits to doubts and
fear in the darkness of the night, she nevertheless uses the striking
image, characteristic of her, of the phosphorous plant, to convey the
support she feels from this traditional symbol of her faith. A total
acceptance of her Christian faith, which is challenged again and again
throughout the cycle, allows her here to express her willingness to
endure whatever Christ places upon her by way of chastisement, and
to reject all alternative inducements.

If I am baptised with Thy sign,
Thou Holy Trinity,
then that will remain with me and cannot move away,
neither in this time nor in that.

Through the frost of reason,
through the foggy course of the human word,
I feel it burning like a clear spark
and gnawing away at the old rust.

It will stir within Thy temple,
where I appeared as Thy handmaid,
and beneath the benediction of Thy priest
I feel it softly deriving sustenance.
When a beloved mother's hand
draws the Cross upon my forehead,
life starts up within my brain,
and my senses are on fire.

Yes, even at night, when all are sleeping,
and fear lays itself upon me,
and when doubt carries its banner
into the harbour of my thoughts,
I sense it still like a phosphorous plant
swelling warm and radiant,
and over the turbulent waves
a gentle shimmering light stretches itself out in spite of everything.

And if the plant of life, which is my companion
and which I missed out on like no other
and set side by side with parched wood,
must suffice to be my judgment,
nevertheless under the spell of sin
and the dazzling bustle of the spirit
it has remained my secret treasure,
and my heart hangs tremulously upon it.

Though I may cower before Thy whip,
nothing is equal to the knowledge
that even so I bear Thy sign
and bleed beneath Thy stroke.
Cursed be everything that pushes me away from Thee!
I will be Thine, derive from Thee alone.
Much rather that Thou shouldst damn me
than that another one should save me.

On Corpus Christi

It is the nature of this extraordinary cycle that completely
contrasting poems are placed side by side, according, of course, to
the Gospel readings which prompt them but also, we can be sure,
reflecting the fluctuations in Droste-Hülshoff's thinking, and even
at times the confusion which appears to have accompanied her
throughout her life and never to have been permanently resolved.
Thus, this next poem, for Corpus Christi, is quite different, in its
complicated thought, from the simple statement of belief in the
sign of baptism which immediately precedes it. Inspired by the
words of St John which record Christ's reply to the Jews who
question the whole idea of the Son of God's offering His very body
as sustenance to those who believe in Him (John 6, 55-58), the
poem also gains greatly in significance because we know that
Droste-Hülshoff was deeply devoted to the idea of the Eucharist
and engaged in debate with Levin Schücking about it. Her letter
to him dated 5 May 1842, admittedly after the writing of this poem,
clearly reflects her central thoughts on the subject: 'I have never
doubted its healing power, and the belief in its sacredness often
comes upon me like an irresistible force.' Brought up in a devout
Catholic family, she appears to have held to its traditions, strangely
enough when the very basis, faith itself, was often an elusive source
of certainty. It is hardly surprising that she was anxious about the
reactions of her family, and that Christoph Schlüter, a most
devoted friend and sincere admirer, confessed to finding her
extremely difficult to understand.

The very idea of Communion, the partaking of the flesh of the
Saviour, is puzzling enough, and Droste-Hülshoff is doing no more
than many who have anguished over the significance of this central
tenet, which has even divided the Church itself. In her case, she

sees her dilemma as another example of the clash within her
between faith and reason. Overriding this, however, is the
tempering belief in the mercy of God, expressed as a reality here,
where in other cases she simply clings to the hope.

Ah, take heart. He is close to you!
Have you not partaken of His Body
and His sacred Blood?
Ah, my poor soul, take heart,
for He is yours. He has become your flesh and your blood.

To be sure, I did not approach His Supper,
as I should have done, rich and warm.
I was a poor, ragged stranger,
yet in me trembled
the torment of longing. Countless tears

have I shed in the fear
which even so was a tremor of joy.
Speak: why are you so afraid
of the medication, so pure and sweet,
that holds out life to you, and peace?

Truly it is terrible to unite one's God
with one's own sinful body.
It sounds like mockery.
Oh, Lord, I am a weak and muddled woman,
and my body is stronger than my soul.

Thus, burdened with guilt,
I have joined myself with Thee in my sins,
and yet Thou hast cried to me
as loudly as to one who weeps for life.
Thus that which shines from above is Grace.

And if Thou hast placed before me
as a test the curse of reason,
it is a deception.
And yet Thou Thyself, Thou Lord of the World,
hast indeed given me the seducer as my companion.

Thus I believe that Thou wilt not
forget this on that Day,
and that Thy Judgment
will say to me: "I overlook the errors.
Your heart was willing, only your head was weak."

On the Second Sunday after Whitsun

In *Luke* 1, 16-24 Christ speaks of the nobleman who prepares a great feast and issues invitations to people who, each in his own way, make excuses for not accepting. Angry, the host tells his servants to go out and summon the lame and the blind, the poor and the maimed, and when the tables are still not filled, he further bids them to go out again 'into the highways and hedges' and compel people to come, for those who were originally summoned and refused will not taste of his feast. Those who would be His disciples, Jesus concludes, must be prepared to forsake everything to follow Him. The message of the Gospel story is clear enough, but what Droste-Hülshoff does with it is characteristically personal, linking as she does the idea of earthly possessions and her vocation as a poet.

> I have bought a house, I have taken a wife,
> and so, Lord, I cannot come.
> The house my earthly frame
> that I must tend in peace,
> my wife poetry,
> at whose feet I will lay
> the product of my love,
> as a sweet pastime.
>
> My house is fragile, in urgent need of repair
> if it is to continue to be of use to me.
> My wife is so delightful

and draws me immeasurably
to behold her beauty.
Ah, I can truly leave to her
the lightning of bright hours,
the heavenly dew of dreams.

What do I feel springing up so hot within my breast,
as if it were wanting to break it to pieces?
What is whispering in my ear?
It seems to me as if a voice
were forcing its way out of the edifice,
as though in suppressed rage,
like the waves of an angry sea
and saying: "Ah, fool, you fool!"

You have not bought a house; it is only leased to you
until that thread ends
whose length no one knows
and no one can make longer.
The spindle rolls and runs.
Ah, no one has yet turned away
the thrust of that hour,
however deeply fear may burn in him.

The woman is not charming: she is a fierce norn.
Tremble before her anger;
she will consume your life,
and if that must run away from you,
make the best purchase:
you can surely gain for yourself
that which in rapture will outweigh
the thorns of all suffering. (f.1)

Therefore do not fret any longer about the walls of your house.
The owner's hands are laid
protectively upon them.
Bargain like a moneylender
for that which moves your heart,

and with that wife transform
the offering into the breath of heaven
which stretches across the abyss/ which bears you upwards. (f.2)

(f.1) This is an instance where it is appropriate to draw attention to the marked difference in this final line between manuscripts. This translation follows the version adopted by Woesler in his edition, but the alternative to 'thorns of suffering' would have been a phrase which seems to express something diametrically opposed to it, 'wellsprings of joy'. It is clear that Droste-Hülshoff played around with the language of her poems, changing, sometimes frequently, small details of her choice of wording, but there were other times when, as here, she actually thought and re-thought the ideas themselves. At this late stage of her life, moreover, we cannot always be sure what she would have intended for a final, published version.
(f.2) In this case, both alternatives are supplied in the translation, since the difference in meaning is less significant and does not seem to require particular comment, but this was clearly a poem to which she returned on more than one occasion.

On the Third Sunday after Whitsun

The Gospel reading on which this poem is based tells of the rich man and the beggar Lazarus, who both die and receive very different treatment in the afterlife, the beggar taken to heaven, into the bosom of Abraham, and the rich man, who has had so much good fortune in the world, destined to endure the torments of hell. Droste-Hülshoff is unsparing in her suggestion of the suffering of the rich man who has been indifferent to the pain of the poor in life, but what makes this poem so typical of her, and links it with others in the cycle and elsewhere, is her description in the second strophe and after it, of her personal isolation and sense of alienation, particularly in the lines which speak of her lonely vigil during the long hours of night, and her appeal to those she calls her 'dead ones'. The poem is immensely bleak and seems to hold out none of the hope that sometimes lifts other poems out of despair. The God of this poem appears to be the vengeful God of the Old Testament, exacting punishment from those who have erred in this life.

One of the most striking features of this extraordinary cycle is the fluctuations in Droste-Hülshoff's mood, and the variations in her concept of God and of her faith, and these features combine to offer a contradictory, challenging and sometimes deeply troubling picture. Clemens Heselhaus concludes his authoritative and thought-provoking essay (1950), by quoting the lines 'We shall fight out the battle/ and leave the power to fate.' More than all other attempts to interpret *Das Geistliche Jahr*, he suggests, they offer a key to her profoundly Christian and human attitude. This is a bold claim, and one may not necessarily accept it, but, coming from someone who knows and understands Droste-Hülshoff so well, it is an idea to be considered very closely.

> But Abraham spoke to the rich man
> and said: "And if they never heard Moses,
> nor the company of prophets,
> then in truth they will never believe
> if a dead man stands before them."
> Then the screen was put in place
> and eternity engraved its silent sign
> upon the tombstone.
>
> How fervently beseeching
> have I so often turned in many a night
> to my dead ones,
> how waited for the passing of many an hour,
> when the land lay grey and whirling in mist!
> And never a sign came to me,
> no crackling sound close to my bed,
> no shimmer of light passing along the walls.
>
> And yet many a time
> I found it hard and loveless
> that that to which I was so passionately inclined
> had not a sound for me in my torment,
> not even a faint sign.
> In their place, it seemed to me,
> I would have ventured everything, all,
> to soothe the wounds of my beloved one.

You could not ever do it!
We shall fight out the battle
and leave the power to fate.
I feel it indeed: the cramp of the soul
must pass away with the night.
Yes: with the last misty dream
the foam of evil must float away,
and thus truth remains nothing but a shimmer.

Oh, in this grey and miserable life,
where shadows lurk over the light,
may only the burning of the pure torch of love
remain for us.
Then we are not deserted either.
And, like the ship on the open sea,
may our boat make its way to harbour,
trusting in the nearness of Pharos. (f)

The terrible condemnation
spoke not a word of the anguish of despair
to the rich man.
No, only the unbroken bread
as the poor and the sick lay groaning
before his house:
only this, weighing down upon him like a millstone,
swept him away to agony and exile.

This is the passage:
"And when he came into torments,
he raised his eyes
and saw in the distance Abraham
surrounded by the holy choir,
with Lazarus in his bosom,
free of pustules, released from agony"
But he – he was in hell.

(f) Pharos: a very early example of a lighthouse, built on the island of Pharos, off the coast of Alexandria, by Ptolemy II in about 280 B.C.

On the Fourth Sunday after Whitsun

From the bleak message of the parable of the rich man and the beggar, the mood changes abruptly with this poem for the Fourth Sunday after Whitsun, for which the Gospel reading is the gentle message of redemption contained in St Luke's account of Christ's response to the Pharisees who criticize His practice of consorting with sinners (*Luke* 15, 1-7). The parable takes its substance, as so often, from the familiar, with His question 'What man of you, having an hundred sheep, if he lose one of them, does not leave the ninety and nine in the wilderness and go after that which is lost until he find it?' The message is the conciliatory, loving one: the lost sheep, the sinner, is brought home by the man rejoicing, and Jesus concludes with a further message which underlines the value of repentance: 'I say unto you, that likewise joy shall be in heaven over one sinner that repenteth, more than over ninety and nine just persons which need no repentance.'

The poem is gentle, too, full of hope and faith, and, despite the characteristic questioning tone, secure. References to the Gospel for the day are barely implied, certainly not explicit, and yet the message of the poem, like that of the words of Christ as reported by St Luke, is clear.

> Thus from the light of Thy holy Book
> a ray has fallen into my night,
> into the mould-grey shaft of my heart.
> Thou gavest it, Lord, Thou hast brought it Thyself to me,
> that which is the jewel of my hope eternally.
>
> It is too much, too much: I can hardly take hold of it.
> Around my totally sunken soul, alas,
> as barren and ashen as the Sea of Gomorrah,
> around that shall be joy in Thy heights.
> It is too much, woe unto me! It is a dream.

Can out of tears, like the arm of the polyp,
the lost essence grow again?
Does remorse restore my strength to me?
Is it enough when passion lies eaten up
as though by a swarm of insects?

Is it enough, before Thy grace and love,
if the hand stretches out yearning and beseeching
over the burned-out building,
the hand which banished all evils,
the hand on which, alas, the burning sign remained?

And yet Thou hast sent forth a holy word,
binding us with the powerful duty of grace
to believe against our own judgment
that which bursts groaning out of the chambers of the heart
and itself recognizes its guilt.

To believe, ah, how sweet and ah, how heavy!
Alas, I may not gaze upon my sins,
shall not suffocate trust in their mud,
like a wild beast in the horror of the swamp,
like a bird upon the Dead Sea.

Lord: who can boldly master that which Thou hast spoken?
Art Thou more merciful than human thought can measure?
Then art Thou, Lord, the Saviour and the Christ,
and I, who am only a dim shadow,
what can I do but kneel, believing?

On the Fifth Sunday after Whitsun

Christ's famous words about those who see the mote in their brother's eye but not the beam in their own (*Luke* 6, 41) are contained within a much longer passage about humility and the deeds of men and the relationship of both with God, and Droste-Hülshoff seizes upon this general message for a poem which is highly introspective and self-analytical. Yet in this case there is again a gentler approach, for there is evidence of confidence in the mercy of a loving God, and every sign that she has faith in Him.

A chasm has opened up
before the eye of my soul.
The course of my life stands withered,
however much I may conceal it from myself.
Yet Truth breaks all veils.
Ah, woe is me: I have not love.

Many a time my heart
has clung to it in desperation,
when my countless sins
pressed in upon me:
this is really true, is not a dream.
My loving is nothing but mist and foam.

Yes, if salvation is still to come to you,
you my immortal being,
you must look straight into the mirror,
must read without flinching
the dark writing in your breast.
Better by far a dagger than seeping poison!

Cold as death – woe unto you! -
you can refuse aid
when only a flourishing little twig
seems to rise up in joy before you:
you who are pricked by the mote of your neighbour
and do not see your own beam!

Who thinks of you as rich? Is it not only
the poor man who bows down?
Have you never bent gently
before joyous nature?
Humbly only and full of misery,
they have extorted the base tribute from you.

It did not occur to you of your own free-will
that if the lips are silent,
if the right hand shows itself gently
in the guise of tender humility,
there is no sweeter display of arrogance
than the self-awareness of one's own goodness.

You did not of your own free-will sense
how your nerves compelled you,
when as fire plays as by electricity,
the alien shudders pressed
into the fragile structure of your body
to become the dew of common, earthly tears.

Take hold, it is high time,
take hold with brave hands.
The scales of the judge are ready.
Your course will soon come to an end.
Does not every breath reveal
how short your path is?

How very wretched I am, and how weak!
Never before did I sense this
until the final support broke
in these difficult hours.
Yet there is One, One after all,
the One can save me yet.

So, Thou barrier against all sins,
Thou dearest of all friends,
do not permit me to fall unheeded
like a soggy, mouldy tree-trunk.
Oh, Highest Power, allow a drop of sap
to run through my veins,

in order that at the very end
I may rank with the living
and precisely not ally myself,
despairing, with the dead.
A drop for the empty veins,
Thou art in truth a sea of all mercies.

CHAPTER SEVEN

On the Sixth Sunday after Whitsun

St Luke's account of the miracle of the abundant catch of fish after
a whole night when none were caught seems to have only a tenuous
link with this poem, although it begins and ends with verbal echoes
of the Gospel: *Luke* 5, 5: 'And Simon answering said unto him:
Master, we have toiled all the night and have taken nothing'; *Luke*
5,10: 'And Jesus said unto Simon, Fear not; from henceforth thou
shalt catch men.'

The poem is, as so often, about her anguished search for faith,
and the burden of remorse and guilt that rests upon her. The idea
of the pearl as the object of intense desire and searching recalls her
poem 'Der Dichter', written just a little later, where the pearl is the
symbol of the vocation of the poet, sought and found at great cost,
even the cost of the soul itself. Here the pearl, achieved and
brought into land in the net, appears to symbolize the achievement
of the peace of religious faith. The two things, faith and her
profound sense of her vocation as a poet, often appear to be
inseparable in her mind. The poem is a notable example of how
Droste-Hülshoff can use a familiar biblical account in a highly
personal way, to produce a poem of intense originality and passion.

I have fished the whole night
for a pearl in the depths of my heart
and caught nothing.
Who has so confounded my being
that desire stands up against desire at all times
in my breast like doves up against snakes?

That I should like to follow Thee, ah,
that is really true,
and I can say it to myself without deceit.

What is creeping behind me then in ghostly fashion
and, as though by the wings holding back the flight
which should bear me to Thee –ah!- to Thee?

Lord, leave me: I am a poor
and all too sinful being. Release me,
ah, leave me lying here!
Do I know what warms my breast?
Is it the glow of yearning, or does mere suffering
make the pulses fly so hot and tremblingly?

When sin defeats itself,
when out of the need for salvation grows yearning,
who will praise it?
Hast Thou not after all placed the judge
in our blood which froths up against sin,
so that it may release itself from the barren sludge.

This swirling known to everyone
when any breath of life still rises up,
will it avail me?
Yes: when the fire of the sun is extinguished,
Egypt has bowed before Thee,
and its sin was not taken from it. (f)

And if perhaps Thou hast not sharpened
the thorn of conscience for me as for others,
then I will atone for it
if the right thrust does not penetrate
which gives freedom to the warm, pure sea,
from which flow the genuine tears of remorse.

Oh, only a real pearl
from the stone-covered fount of my eyes:
that would be a blessing.
Thou master of all nature,
break in, Thou rescuer, release the bright streams!
Without Thee, I can truly never move.

Thou who hast said: "Fear not",
let me trust in Thy hand
and not grow weary.
Yes, over Thy word, my light of hope,
I will throw my net. Ah, will then the pearl
at last rise on to the land and bring me peace?

(f) Exodus 10, 21-29

On the Seventh Sunday after Whitsun

It is the concept of reconciliation that links this poem with the Gospel reading. *Matthew* 5, 23-24 tells how Jesus told His disciples: 'Therefore if thou bring thy gift to the altar, and there rememberest that thy brother hath ought against thee, leave there thy gift before the altar and go thy way; first be reconciled to thy brother and then come and offer thy gift.' As so often Droste-Hülshoff accuses herself, burdened with the memory of past sins, yet unable to recall the nature of those sins. Only in the closing strophe does she hold out the hope that God, the Merciful One, will forgive.

The poem is rich in images: of the ship riding the waves in the fourth strophe, with the additional details of the abandoned harbour, the plumb-bob, and the cliffs looming in the distance; the worn-out coat of the fifth strophe, and there, too, the image of the trailing plant with its tendrils and the harvest, associated here not with fruition but with a curse. The remainder of the poem is filled with the image of a rushing stream, the threat of being swept away, yet the power of God to stem the force of the thrusting water, in order to prevent the catastrophe of the whirlpool. Overall is the image of the hand outstretched in reconciliation, her own hand towards those she has unwittingly wronged, the hand of one human being to another, and the merciful hand of God. It is characteristic of some of these late religious poems that she passes through turbulence and anguish, in order to arrive at a gentle conclusion, supported by faith achieved and the confidence in a forgiving God.

Where are you, you who are still unreconciled with me?
I will gladly stretch out my hand, joyfully, towards you.
I do not know what wrong I have done you.
Gone are the old times, old signs.
Years have run away from me like a dream,
and I barely turn my thoughts backwards
to images which grow pale like cloudy shadows.

Out of harsh anguish and many a bitter battle
a new life has dawned for me,
no joyful one: I sense the fiery inner cramp,
less captured now from outside.
The gaze boring forcefully inside
can now penetrate deeper, more deeply,
into the dark crevice of the long crusted wounds.

That which moves me has gone, blown away;
long since departed are those who came together once,
and like a ship which rides the sea,
completely forgetting the once abandoned harbour,
I let the plumb-bob drop trembling to the depths
to find out where the soul is sick and wounded
and where –ah, woe!- the hidden cliffs are sleeping.

Ah, can I then brush away from me like this
things done, like a worn-out coat?
Is a man himself only ever happy about his sadness
when a thousand little threads of the trailing plants
which he has sown grasp at him,
when everywhere the harvest of the curse is,
everywhere the crazed sighs wander?

Oh, shake yourself, open your eyes!
Once again you must turn them towards the outside,
must see the spring as the wild course of the stream

which you have opened up with your hands.
And where it was stemmed by the grace of God,
there beat upon your breast in your guilt,
and do not imagine that you could accomplish anything.

Yes, if I only turn my gaze backwards,
then I know where I must beg for mercy,
where I am beholden to exchange the happiness
of my own life for the agonies of an alien soul.
Then do I know indeed who, still not reconciled with me,
scorns perhaps my outstretched right hand,
allows me to pass uncomforted according to my deserts.

Where I have deceived in recklessness or arrogance,
there first may I perchance be pardoned,
but where a pure blood was poisoned,
a life surrendered to an alien example,
there lies the stone which my sinful hand
was too skilled, alas, in casting,
yet now is much too weak to lift from the ground.

Merciful One, ah, do not any longer allow the course of sin
to drive me so powerfully towards the whirlpool!
Look, I raise my hands in fear:
do not leave me so terrible a monument!
I shall in truth not be ashamed of late penitence:
so send to these people also Thy clear light
that, shuddering, they may avoid the chasm.

My God, I surely do not beg for pardon,
to steal for myself love undeserved.
Go to them, Lord, be near only to them.
Whatever other pain torments me, in this world and the next,
Thou merciful One, only not this one thing,
that I before Thy eternal Judgment
must see a single soul lost because of me.

On the Eighth Sunday after Whitsun

This is a rather unusual example of a poem for which Droste-Hülshoff uses a Gospel story in a fairly straightforward way. Christ's feeding of the five thousand from the five loaves and two fishes is probably one of the most familiar stories (*Mark*, 8, 1-9) and the miracle has an immediacy which Droste-Hülshoff does not disguise. Only in the middle strophes does she depart from the simple narrative to link this event to herself, and to use the idea of hunger and sustenance in an obviously symbolic way, to refer to the craving of the soul for nourishment from a kindly God. In accordance with the relative simplicity of thought is the relatively uncomplicated language.

> The crowd was totally exhausted,
> and to be sure the pangs of hunger were gnawing at them.
> Then didst Thou loyally pay heed to them.
> Ah, hast Thou not,
> after years of drought and heat,
>
> a bite to eat, a refreshing drink,
> for the weary, empty soul,
> no fresh breath of grace,
> which might cool the seething brain
> in the fire and toil of the desert?
>
> For behold, I came indeed from afar,
> even if I had sent myself into exile.
> Thou art standing no less close to me because of that.
> Anyone who has once turned to Thee
> with senses newly awakened,
>
> anyone who has once taken refuge beneath Thy roof,
> away from the yoke of the driver,
> even if that person is so cowered,

Thou art so gentle and do not hold
the calluses of the whip of slavery against him.

Oh, save me, in order that the deceit of hunger
cannot oppress me,
that I may not stretch out my hands
under the curse of madness
and seize the poisonous fruit on its withered stem,

(the fruit) which is called knowledge
and which drove them out of paradise.
If like a thief it steals life,
it nevertheless tempts the burning gums
with the playful touch of juice that seems refreshing.

Ah, the desert lies not near me
but within my breast.
Where then can I find, where can I find here
that which does not deceive my hunger,
that which will rinse my parched throat?

Thus also did Thy disciples speak,
and Thou, merciful One, after all found bread,
where the breath of the scorching samum
offered Thee no ear of corn, but only sand and whirling dust.

"There they ate and were filled,
and gathered up that which was left over."
No one was ill any more, no one weary,
and the recovered man became dear to Thee,
as dear as the many healthy ones.

On the Ninth Sunday after Whitsun

Very different from the preceding poem is this one, which is based
on the passage from the Sermon on the Mount in which Jesus
warns of the false prophets: 'Beware of false prophets which come

to you in sheep's clothing, but inwardly they are ravening wolves. Ye shall know them by their fruits. Do men gather grapes of thorns, or figs of thistles? Even so every good tree bringeth forth good fruit; but a corrupt tree bringeth forth evil fruit. A good tree cannot bring forth evil fruit, neither can a corrupt tree bring forth good fruit. Every tree that bringeth not forth good fruit is hewn down, and cast into the fire. Wherefore by their fruits ye shall know them. Not every one that saith unto me, Lord, lord, shall enter into the kingdom of heaven; but he that doeth the will of my Father which is in heaven.' (*Matthew* 7, 15-21)

This time Droste-Hülshoff is struggling with her faith in a very personal way, rejecting alternative forms of faith in the third, fourth, fifth and sixth strophes before arriving in the final three at the gentle, genuine faith which offers hope and sustenance. This often eludes her, of course, but here she reaches a belief characterised by humility, to describe which she uses the familiar motifs of a meal which satisfies all her needs, the Holy Grail and the temple. The sense of relief and release is summed up in the final line, which holds out the promise of the passing of the storm. Briefly, she appears to have reached some kind of final place, but, as we know from the cycle as a whole, this can only be temporary for this anguished mind.

One need only take the poems for the Eighth and Ninth Sundays after Whitsun to illustrate the extraordinary range of thought and mood in this cycle but, of course, fluctuations in her thinking and her mood are totally characteristic of the whole and account to a high degree for its impact, and, one might almost say, for the fact that it could never truly be viewed as complete. The last word is never uttered in *Das Geistliche Jahr*.

Oh beware, beware!
The air has clouded over
and in the vivid, richly coloured clouds
a false arch of peace is rising,
out of which a demon descended,
bringing war along with the olive branch.

And on all sides stand
trumpeting prophets
who are making ropes out of the dust
and want to tread the mountains flat underfoot.
Oh, beware, their faces are honourable
and their beards are grey.

One points to the chasm
where the divine Acropolis
of the Christian Minerva
is said to stand on naked heights.
If you follow him you will remain banished
where no tiny blade of grass ever found nourishment.

There you may sink to your knees
in prayer before arid stone,
and for a long time afterwards your bones
will radiate a cautionary tale,
as of One who for His own needs
turned bread into stone.

The other points far down
into the depths of a cave,
and, in his delusion, seems to hear
a voice crying to him out of the abyss:
"This way!" But that is clearly an illusion:
in the mineshaft dwells the precious stone.

Oh, do not follow this one
who makes the house of God into a shrine,
and- woe!- do not follow that one
who turns God's food into stone.
Yet it is better to stand mouldering in the shaft
than to gaze straight up towards the sky.

And in the green field
where the fresh plants grow, abundantly,
the way leads so bright with dew
and the lively streams sparkle
and out of the grey stone of humility
a temple rises up, straight and small.

There you will find a meal,
exactly as you need it;
there you may sup gentle refreshment
from the Holy Grail of faith,
exactly as befits a creature
who is still the servant of the earthly body.

Oh, only restrain your ear
which is surrounded by strange noises!
Oh, do not look upwards in desire
towards the brightly coloured, false arch of peace.
You should kneel at your temple.
The storm will pass over.

On the Tenth Sunday after Whitsun

This rather puzzling poem is based on the already-puzzling Gospel
reading from St Luke, which has Christ commending His disciples
to the service of Mammon. The meaning, however, emerges more
clearly, for what He is saying is that money - material possessions -
is not evil in itself: what is evil is man's obsession with it to the
exclusion of spiritual things. The injunction follows immediately
upon the parable of the unjust steward, who, knowing that he was
to be dismissed from his master's employment, saw to it that he had
stored up wealth for himself against that day. (*Luke*, 16, 1-9). The
message is not a commendation of wealth but a reminder that
accruing material wealth in this world may be the foundation of a
life to come of spiritual riches. As Christ continues 'He that is

faithful in that which is least is faithful also in much: and he that is unjust in the least is unjust also in much', and the passage concludes with the famous statement: 'No servant can serve two masters, for either he will hate the one and love the other; or else he will hold to the one and despise the other. Ye cannot serve God and mammon.' True riches are achieved by the one who loves God, and it is this ultimate message of the Gospel passage which Droste-Hülshoff seems to be reiterating throughout the poem, which touches also on her sense of the value of her vocation and the obligation she has, before God, to honour it.

Thus she links images of wealth and money-lenders, of accruing interest and storing up gold, with more abstract references to the 'gold of words' and the 'empty fame' which, as we know from other occasions in her work, was not of importance to her. It is not an easy poem to comprehend, but it fits in with her highly contemplative analysis within this cycle of her destined role and her obligation to God. It is another outstanding example of how she can move from the prescribed reading to a very broad interpretation.

> Why hast Thou commended to me
> the unrighteous Mammon, according to Thy will?
> Not in order that, a shiny trinket,
> it shall envelope gnawed imperfections,
> nor to fill the fleeting hours in this world
> with fresh earthly delight.
> No: quite otherwise.
> Ah, that which Thou givest is not so empty and hollow.
>
> With Thy blessing I shall profiteer
> with its brightly-coloured rays.
> For my hunger I shall enter a meal
> into the eternal reckoning,

and for my nakedness, limp and pale,
it shall be a warm coat,
when that time breaks in when
that which is not mine scatters and rusts away.

Then I shall be sick and quite impoverished,
then will the bitter deprivation come
when that on which my heart has warmed itself grows icy cold,
and that from which I took my solace disperses like dust,
if Thy hand does not take pity
and still point in gentleness to my advantage
towards the penny secreted away against that time.

Do not leave me, Lord, in that awesome hour
to fall down weeping for aid,
that hour which stands before me like the night of chaos,
as darkness floods over darkness.
Alas for me, I have not thought of it!
So let me from this time on be aware of it
above all things.
Oh, touch me with gentleness or anguish!

Let me henceforth dispense the gold of words
with the care of the money-lender,
in order that when now today rolls away,
tomorrow is not lost to me.
Let me be mindful that the pay
I had to borrow from empty fame
was taken from the golden treasury for past and present.

And let me but behold a quill
with secret trembling,
remembering that life and death
softly slipping past follow the black trail.
Oh Lord, let me be relieved of the interest
on the pounds that nature gave to me.
I am so poor and only warm inside the borrowed fur.

Oh God, how heavy is my heart,
compressed by dawning understanding!

Can the splendid gifts be given
as noble pledges to me?
Oh, just a single little drop to me
from the edge of the sea of Thy wisdom
and with this drink
the gall itself must turn to honey.

On the Eleventh Sunday after Whitsun

This moving poem takes as its focus the words of St Luke when he speaks of how Jesus approaches Jerusalem shortly before the momentous events leading up to His Crucifixion, and, when He beholds it, weeps (*Luke* 19,41). From this single verse, which she describes as the one which moves her most deeply in the whole of the Bible, Droste-Hülshoff creates this very personal statement of her belief in the love of God for her, a weak and helpless human being close to despair, yet never really doubting the mercy of God. As so often, there is the awareness of her vocation, that the 'little treasures' she possesses can be given to God who will receive them and, in return, grant that love she so desires. The poem is filled with the sense of her own inadequacy, the poorest beggar dreaming of salvation, compared with St Veronica, on whom Christ bestowed the gift of his countenance on the sacred cloth. She is an arid piece of land, which cannot be nourished by the traditional means of fertilization, the ashes and burnt chalk. Yet still, in this parched state, weary unto death, she hopes for the sustenance of heavenly water.

One recalls the early poems, with the desperate craving for the love of God, and one sees that this theme is still dominant now that her life is nearing its close, and when, in other poems of this time, she appears to show an almost robust optimism. Even here, there is hopefulness, sustained by the theme of the weeping of

Christ for His city of Jerusalem, but ultimately for the soul of the individual to which, coming to its close, the poem returns.

My Jesus wept for His city,
and ah! certainly He also wept for me.
Did He not then already know how wretched and feeble,
how helpless, my soul appears today?
Of all that the Holy Bible imparts,
nothing has moved me so deeply, so poignantly.

Ah, if only I might catch His precious tears
in a chalice, in a cloth, just as He wished to leave for Veronica
the sacred traces of His bloody countenance!
She was the most highly blessed of the Lord,
yet the poorest beggar also likes to dream.

I should gladly place in such a chalice
whatever little treasures I possess,
and it would become rich and heavy with my gold,
and my precious stones should sparkle.
Oh, Lord, do not be vexed by my foolishness:
Thy goodness makes me today into a child.

"Alas, if only you knew what salvation there is for you!"
Yes, if I knew, it would certainly be to my advantage.
Yet Thou, Thou knowest it indeed, my Jesus Christ,
and only from Thee can the message come to me.
So, speak to me, Thou my heart's treasure.
I stand here and hearken to Thy word.

To be sure, I must rather search in Thy Holy Book
for the signs of Thy love
than where Thy zeal speaks, and, alas, Thy curse.
I bend like a blade of grass if I hear Thee curse.
I lie like a withered leaf upon the earth,
not shaken off in health but weary unto death.

I am an arid piece of ground, which the burning of chalk,
the scorching of ash can do nothing to help.
I follow the wind like parched sand;

thus will I suck Thy heavenly drops
and in that drink Thou wilt perhaps give to me
that which will suffice for my erring consciousness.

Put into my heart that which I must do,
whether to stand grieving or to step forward in hope.
Mercy is not the price of strength
but can float down also to the sick one.
Thou who art the Creator of the very weakest,
my Jesus Christ, hast for him too a means of salvation.

Thus, when the cloud once more enfolds me
and when my arms grow weak almost in desperation,
then will I remember that He has loved
and raise my eyelids through the shadows.
Ah, my soul, do not be so hard as stone:
you know for sure that He has wept for you.

On the Twelfth Sunday after Whitsun

This next poem returns to another familiar theme, recurrent in her
youth and never truly put aside: the obsession with guilt. It is
evoked in this case, again, by the reading from *St Luke*, which
contrasts the behaviour of the Pharisee and the publican as they
pray in the temple. The Pharisee offers thanks to God that he is
not as other men are, whereas the publican simply asks God for
mercy on him, sinful man that he knows himself to be (18, 9-14).
Christ concludes: 'every man that exalteth himself shall be abased;
and he that humbleth himself shall be exalted.' Again, Droste-
Hülshoff expresses herself in relatively simple terms, as she speaks
of her awareness of guilt and her appeal for divine mercy,
culminating in the final lines which very closely echo the words of
the Gospel.

Yes, when I behold Thy sacrificial flame
in the pure glow of a pious eye,
there is a gleam of light as if it were damning me.
The sharp ray enters my guilty blood.
How the brightness blinds me!
I may not raise my eyes:
I may not do it
and my eyelids tremble.

And beneath the closed eye-lids
the shades of bye-gone sins move to and fro,
and then may that which reveals itself to my mind
not be so grievous to my foe!
They steam from the floor and walls, too,
float through the rooms,
images made of smoke.
Thus it was and always will be.

Whenever I see a kindly deed performed,
completely from the depths of an overflowing heart,
warm springs of love spurting up so clear,
asking only what may be good for one's brother;
whenever a gentle tear,
a very child of God,
glints on the robe of mercy,
and does not ask why it is weeping,

then does my conscience burrow away within my breast,
and rubbish and debris is my one achievement.
Bestowing and striving are torn from me
out of the thorns of brooding as though bereft of simplicity.
Yes: everywhere my foot kicks
against the grating, against the criss-cross planks of my prison,
and trembling
I must beat my breast.

Ah, above all, when a pious voice
whispers to me a simple, holy word,
so certain that my heart swims in faith,
so unconcerned around the harbour of my life,
offers the sound of Thy grace
guiltless as the sign of resolution,

and full of trust wishes
to slide into my breast,

then must all the words rise up
that I have ever spoken sinfully,
and everything that can still disturb me
rises up and whirls around me like a lake,
then to this day I feel myself in the foam
not freed from any bonds
and then I can barely moan:
may God be merciful to me, sinner that I am!

On the Thirteenth Sunday after Whitsun

In this powerful reflection of *St Mark* 7, 31-37, Droste-Hülshoff
allies herself with the deaf man inflicted also with a severe speech
impediment, who is cured by Jesus at the Sea of Galilee with the
single instruction 'Be opened', rendered here, as in the Gospel, by
the Greek 'Ephephata'. For Droste-Hülshoff this is not simply a
restoring of two impaired senses, for, just as the deaf and dumb were
deemed to be weak-minded, so she sees herself as cursed by this
affliction, separated from those words which are by rights her
kinsmen, and paralysed by the double affliction. Like the preceding
poems, this is a deeply personal statement which links her own
suffering with the Gospel story and finds a way forward by means
of its message.

Touch my tongue:
Thou canst release it.
Break the spell on my ear,
and I shall be cured.
No, I am not lost, gentle God,
although I may be crushed, the object of my enemy's mockery.
I cry to Thee, Thou faithful One, fight Thou against the evil one!

He has paralysed
the threads of my nerves.
Words enter
only through the doorway of my eyes,
when the heart would wish to turn around within my breast
as it seizes the divine pleasure of pious ways,
and the hidden hurts would wish to bleed to death.

Thus, after all,
I am not altogether lost,
as long as some life
still presses its way towards me,
and even if only, as in the forehead of a madman,
the slumbering brain stirs softly.
It lives, and I may hope, even as I tremble.

Only words, words are not
kinsmen of mine.
As the wind crashes down
from the edge of the mountain, so does that which
touches others and frightens others crash down
that crust which covers my brain
and which I once called a sentry and a wall.

It is not always so.
Sometimes from the kingdom
of the sounds
mighty signs slip forth,
as a tear forces its way out of a heart,
as the chasm of the mountain takes up the distant thunder.
Ah, then I feel myself grow pale with joy.

No: my lips
cannot express
how tears break
from the depths.
No: that which flows so strangely into the soul
has not yet loosened the bonds of my tongue,

runs only half comprehended in warm streams.
Oh, powerful treasure,
place Thy merciful hands
upon the opening of my ear!
Oh, turn the peaceful pleading of Thy gaze around me
also upwards and say "Ephephata"
then it will come to pass,
then shall I be free and then the curse shall be at an end.

On the Fourteenth Sunday after Whitsun

This poem is based on Christ's response to the lawyer who asks Him
what he must do to inherit eternal life (*Luke*, 10, 23-37): 'Thou
shalt love the lord thy God with all thy heart, and with all thy soul,
and with all thy strength and with all thy mind, and thy neighbour
as thyself'. The lawyer persists with his questioning, demanding to
know who is his neighbour, which elicits by way of response from
Jesus the parable of the Good Samaritan, the story which above all
advocates undiscriminating charity towards a fellow human being.
Droste-Hülshoff echoes the lawyer's question in her opening line,
and the poem widens also into a meditation on human love and
friendship, the abandonment of petty dislikes and criticisms and
even hatred, and love as the basis of true faith: the 'right stone', as
she calls it, for the building of a proper relationship with God. This
is a plea for tolerance in everyday human dealings, but also, at a
time of conflict and disagreement within the Church, for a benign
understanding of contrasting views.

It is significant that of all the poems of the second part of *Das
Geistliche Jahr*, this is the only one which exists in what may
confidently be described as a final form, approved by the poet herself
when she chose to copy it into the album of her nephew Heinrich,

the much loved son of her brother Werner, who had proved an affectionate and attentive companion to his aunt when she travelled, weak and sick, to Meersburg in 1846. There is abundant evidence of the importance she attached to the ties with family and friends in her letters and the accounts of her contemporaries, but this is a single poignant piece of autobiographical information to add to our understanding of the great cycle, and indeed of the woman herself, at this very late stage of her life.

> Who is it who stands close to me?
> Whom must I call my brother?
> To whom must I grant my most precious gift?
> To whom (must I) give before he even asks?
> Oh, Mighty One, let the dew of Thy wisdom
> drip on to my brow.
> Let me take up the right stone
> for the eternal building of Thy temple.
>
> To him whom the same womb has carried
> and who has suckled at the same breast am I inclined,
> whether I wish to be or not.
> Nothing can tear apart the bonds of blood.
> And he who has breathed the same air,
> drunk at the stream of the same ground,
> for him has nature lit the spark
> in every bosom.
>
> Like him who has knelt at the same altar
> in the bonds of the same faith,
> and where the same direction takes me,
> be it in spirit, be it in mind,
> all these are as if given to me,
> into the protection of my own hearth,
> are all fibres of my life,
> are all drops of my blood.

Yet, when in air far from my home
a wretched creature searches anxiously
to read the writing in strange letters,
when no one calls his name,
then come close and call it only
with each word of love:
then can you burn out the torch
that nature did not ignite.

And when at the gate of your temple
stands a man, alone, shut out,
whose tears have nevertheless flowed in the presence of God,
whose sigh nevertheless reaches His ear,
to such a man may you stretch out your right hand
and point upwards to the blueness,
where the signs of the stars glow for everyone
and the gentle dew falls for all people.

And even when a powerful revulsion stirs in you
towards one person,
because another way is given to him
than heaven has assigned to you,
when error linked with foolishness will stifle
the seed of love,
reach out your hand to him.

This is the moment when the command approaches with a test.
Yes, you must in all gentleness
accustom yourself even to the gaze of the despicable one
who would seek to scorn heaven and earth:
you may shudder with fear but not turn back.
Ah, if you can creep round him in Jesus Christ,
peering at his wounds,
then at last you will have found the stone,
then you will know who is your neighbour.

CHAPTER SEVEN

On the Fifteenth Sunday after Whitsun

This poem focuses on healing, based as it is on the story as related by St Luke (17, 11-19), of the ten lepers who approach Jesus to be healed: only one of them, the Samaritan, gives thanks. However, it is not on this feature of the account that Droste-Hülshoff bases her poem but on the very issue of healing itself. She begins with the instruction of Jesus which commences this miracle: 'Go hence and show yourselves to the priests' (cf. *Luke* 17, 14), but the poem is, of course, about her guilt, the leprosy within her which can be cured only by the Hand of God, and it culminates in the complex image contained in the final two stanzas, which compares the priest who grants Absolution in the Sacrament of Confession with the page on which the soul writes out its guilt. Only God Himself can pronounce freedom from guilt, that little speck of healing which may appear in the leprosy.

Then He said: "Go hence and show yourselves to the priests."
And as they went, behold, they became clean.
You my poor soul, rich only in misery,
great in terms of errors, you could be likewise helped,
you the hand of man, still always despised,
and even if it were sanctified by God and if it were sent by God.

To be sure you often say to yourself in vicious deception:
"He is the powerful One who alone can save me.
If He does not help me, then human counsel is a lie, too.
Let my beseeching rise aloft straightway to Him."
And you do not feel that, warm and richly tended,
arrogance lays its leprosy upon your foolish heart.

Is then your spirit so firm, so rich and strong in faith,
that it may reject the hand of a friend,
your brain so clear, your marrow so supple and so healthy
that your perception is sharp above all other beings?

Oh, be humble, say it openly:
"You live like a beggar and in the house of a beggar."

No matter how poor and weak you are, my soul, you really think
you can feel it, when the mouth speaks wearily and plaintively,
and yet it is nothing but a sound, a rustling, hollow swelling,
as, newly formed, a whisper breaks out from the mouthpiece,
just a cry that escapes involuntarily,
while your dark gaze turns proudly inward on itself.

What is to be seen so glorious in there, then?
A wretched creature that perishes, alas, under its own pressure,
that – in truth- a slave to every charm and every mood,
now stands like a swamp, now flies like a whirlpool,
a brain of which you yourself do not know
whether it is more closely related to madness or to sin.

These are the treasures that have made you proud and strong,
so that you have rejected the counsel of the Creature.
These are the beams of light which, gloriously, are meant to light
the hidden pathway in the night of dull doubt.
And so, and so, you trust alone in God,
that the thorn of human blame may leave you.

Have you ever thought indeed about the priest
who exonerated you from guilt in the Holy Sacrament
as anything other than the page on which the debtor wrote his
account but only recognized the writing of the believer as solution?
Were in his hand ever visible to you the sombre scales
on which your life and death rested?

Kneel down, kneel down, but not in that place of mercy.
No: only before the shepherd in the strength of his dignity!
And may your soul be an open page
in front of him in all its vanity and lowly passion.
And when you have bowed before the human hand, then look to see
if a little speck of healing has not appeared in the leprosy.

On the Sixteenth Sunday after Whitsun

This poem is based, but really rather loosely, on the injunction contained in *St Matthew* 6, 24: 'No man can serve two masters....' but it moves on, somewhat disconnectedly, to the famous passage a little later in the same chapter which urges the true significance of life as being beyond the material and everyday: 'Consider the lilies of the field, how they grow; they toil not, neither do they spin: and yet I say unto you, that even Solomon in all his glory was not arrayed like one of these.' For the final two strophes, she augments this passage with the words of St Luke: 'Consider the ravens, for they neither sow nor reap; which neither have storehouse nor barn, and God feedeth them' (*Luke* 12, 24).

The poem is then ultimately, like so many, a statement of her personal faith, challenged repeatedly yet emerging so often more or less intact.

He who in all his trials
trusts only in the power of God,
that man no enemy has brought to the fall,
no evil can kill him.
And when fear overwhelms him,
the strongest hero of all, the Saviour, will come to his side.

With His sharp spear He will turn
his opponents into dust,
and of the greatest army of all
no hoof-print will remain.
Whether the enemy be without or within,
if only the true hero appears,
He can define its boundaries.

He is the very best lord
that anyone can achieve,
and the labourer who is caught up in His service

has a blessed life.
His slavery is so sweet that anyone,
no matter how free he may be,
may long for it.

The torment of hunger, the shame of nakedness,
He knows how to compensate for them.
No one right up to this day
could accuse Him of being faithless.
With increasing gain He pays all
who have placed their lives and their substance
in His service.

And in His right hand he holds
the talisman of all strength.
Even out of the sharpest thorns
He can weave garlands of roses.
On the wild battlefield
He shows to you the true serpent of Aaron (f)
if you must fight with vipers.

And if the fiercest enemy stirs,
He shows you a sign that,
no matter how bad his intentions,
the dragon must swiftly draw back in face of it.
Only let it be wielded with true belief
by a ready hand,
otherwise it will not suffice.

The man weak in faith and trust,
if he is driven by longing,
may nevertheless see from a distance
that he is in the rear.
Upon him, refreshing in the intense heat,
the gentle shadow of the hero rests,
like the discs of a mighty shield.

Yet no suffering can oppress him
in whom faith is pure and clear.
He can indeed, bereft of all possessions,

still sing like a bird:
"Behold the lilies in the field,
how fresh and well established they are,
how green and flourishing!

"They pay no attention to the spinning
and are so richly adorned
that Solomon in all his glory
merits much less praise.
Yet, behold the young ravens,
how well fed and beautiful they are,
with what smooth and shiny ribbons.

He who nourishes the young ravens
will take care of me, too,
even if He had to make bread for me
out of the cinders in the stove.
Fortunate for me that I gained the Lord
in whose service no one has ever come to harm.
I shall cling to Him."

(f) Exodus 10-12

On the Seventeenth Sunday after Whitsun

The impetus to this poem is the story told by Luke (7, 11-16) of how Jesus raised from the dead the son of the widow at Naim. The single direct quotation from the Gospel is His command to the grieving mother 'Weep not', and the whole poem represents a completely new reflection of the original in terms of the poet herself. She it is who is lying in the coffin, the corpse, her deeds themselves, stained by sin, and longing to be restored to life by the words of the Lord, to be awoken from sleep and allowed to sense again the fragrance of the morning air. As the poem ends, this hope is denied, for she is lying in her shroud still, and the life she craves is not yet given to her. The poem moves between despair and the awareness, so often present in Droste-Hülshoff, of guilt, and the hope that this can yet give way to new life, and the new sounds that she may still utter. This hope, expressed so powerfully in the fifth stanza, links her love of God with her vocation as a poet. Both, she believes, can be released by the touch of the Saviour's hand.

> When Thy hand touches the coffin,
> the dead man must come to life,
> and when Thy breath governs the thunder cloud,
> it must bring forth manna.
> Thou who brought forth nourishment from the rocks
> and for whom Aaron's withered rod blossomed,
> the waters of the Nile rise up.
>
> Thou art the Mighty One,
> who can put an end to the dull sleep of the soul.
> To Thee may the mortally wounded criminal
> send forth his dying breath.
> Thou takest the last breath,
> a whisper of remorse is enough for Thee
> to turn back the flash of lightning in its flight.
>
> Thou hast placed Thyself at the gate
> to await the widow's son and hast,
> Lord of all the world,
> observed her little garden.
> Thou hast come all alone
> to wash our stains clean
> and smooth our blemishes.
>
> Touch me, for I am dead
> and my deeds are but corpses.
> Breathe on me, for sin has left
> its blood-red signs on me.
> Oh, turn away the clap of thunder
> that broke over my head,
> and let the dull mists roll back.

Then I will sing to Thee from my unfettered breast
a rapturous song of praise
and once more in love of God
my voice will resound as it did before.
If it is broken now and dull,
it is Thou who hast the means
to penetrate the weakest veins like this.

If today I nevertheless feel awakened
within me a long vanished hope
that neither death nor sin makes me afraid,
why should I then not build upon Thee?
Yes, if Thou wilt, I can still nevertheless
with these eyes of mine
see Thee in this my body.

I know that that which must shudder through me so joyfully
does not stem from me.
It is a ray which Thou hast enflamed,
a dream to shake the stubborn one.
Oh go on, touch me;
oh, break that sleep of death and then,
then shall I scent the morning air.

If Thou hast said: "Weep not!"
Thou knowest that the dead do not weep,
even if in a dream the heart is almost breaking
and sighs seem indeed to Thee like prayers
that might whisper weakly and gently:
"Thou hast awoken the widow's child,
and I am still lying in a shroud."

On the Eighteenth Sunday after Whitsun

The rhythm of this poem makes it stand out from others of the cycle: it moves with speed and vigour in a way few others do. It is distinctive, too, in the way Droste-Hülshoff uses the biblical echoes, opening with the injunction of the Lord to Moses (*Exodus* 6, 9-10) and only at the end touching on the Gospel for the day, (*Luke* 14, 1-11) which tells of how Christ cured the man afflicted with dropsy, and of His challenge to the Pharisees: 'Is it lawful to heal on the Sabbath day?', to which question they had no answer.

The poem thus becomes a praise of useful activity, as opposed to rigid adherence to the law, and in that respect, too, it is unusual in its presentation of a universal message, rooted in biblical teaching.

Six days shalt Thou do Thy work
faithfully
and shalt rest on the seventh,
which is sanctified by the Lord.
Thus it was ordained for us
and thus we do,
just as the dull beast
greedily wets its beak.

One man celebrates with a game,
another with the bottle,
and each one ponders long and hard
how he may gain his pleasure.
To whom is that denied
which cannot praise the Lord
and which maddens the senses?
Worthy of the Holy Sabbath.

Yes, if one can heap up
the sins of the whole week
compared with the harvest
one must find on this day,
then, ah shame!, it will count
as two ears of corn that one has picked,
compared with the heap
from which the corn rolls.

Do the churches stand empty, then?
Does the sinner flee from his lord?
Ah, if that were only so,

the crime would be less heavy.
Yet out of the waves of incense
which surround our God,
one shoots like a vulture
at the halls of destruction.

In the pledge of the old alliance
when grace was still beginning to germinate
and light was falling only dimly
on the paths of human beings,
the Sabbath did not yet bear
the stains of sin but had to strike fear
into the faithful one,
ah, like an iron yoke.

It may well be foolish,
in honour of the highest God,
to lie like a rock
and resist all movement,
but to surrender the compliant alliance
of the senses to vain desires –
oh, better to lie ten times over
like a clod in the earth!

Thus the Saviour did not
reject the old alliance:
you shall praise the Almighty
by means of deeds like light.
May the poor man be greeted
by you with your generous gift.
The hands from which flows blessing
are not impure.

And if someone moves insignificant and small
in the bed of pain,
where loneliness oppresses him
worse than anguish,
bind up his wounds
and smile while you are doing it.
Then you will have found it,
the true peace of the Sabbath.

On the Nineteenth Sunday after Whitsun

The reading from St Matthew (22, 35-46) contains the central message of Christian faith, given by Jesus in response to the question of the Pharisees: 'Which is the great commandment in the law?' The answer comes: 'Thou shalt love the Lord thy God with all thy heart, and with all thy soul and with all thy mind. This is the first and great commandment. And the second is like unto it. Thou shalt love thy neighbour as thyself.' As is clear from so many of the poems, particularly the earlier ones, this is an issue which concerns Droste-Hülshoff deeply, and she addresses it in forthright terms in the opening lines before setting out the dichotomy which seems to have followed her throughout her life. The poem thus becomes the expression of a personal struggle, and the argument she presents in it a statement of her thinking at this point, and a most significant stage in her development and her progress towards self-understanding. It is, of course, the nature of this cycle that no individual poem ever seems to represent a final conclusion in this development, though the final strophe comes close to holding out the possibility that such a conclusion might be attainable. The complex thought is more than ever reflected here in the complicated, even tortuous, syntax.

I do not know, God,
if I love Thee.
I often think that it is only Thee
whom this breast embraces
full of mercy
and like a redeeming torch
in the radiance of all other love
and dawning longing.

When the spirit soars freely
towards the noblest thing,
that which encircles it as a thought
yet living, invisible
yet not without its essence,
distant yet everywhere,
whose traces speak out of a human eye
and out of the blessing of a tear,

then am I truly consoled
and prayer rises
so confidently from my lips
as if in strange love, or in Thine –
who has ever fathomed it? –
were offered
everything that remained worthy of longing
and proclaims Thy breath.

Yet then at another time
I feel myself consecrated to the dark earth,
like hair to the head,
so robbed of power,
when in a friend the failings,
weaknesses, pressed to my heart,
delight me like a charm,
that no one could steal from me.

So would it only be a sign from God
that I have recognized,
and not that sinful Nature
was holding out her hand,
when I can tolerate
the virtue of my loved ones with reverence,
yet my heart would surely beat
more purely and more coldly?

As the cheek of Damocles grew pale
beneath the sword,
or like one who, on the bank of the river
looks at his reflection, smiles and drinks,

while the treacherous sand is slipping gently away
and his foothold is sinking:
woe! a cold cloud
is passing over me.

Oh, Saviour, Saviour, who suffered also
for the fools,
come to me, before the wave
slides over my head!
Stretch out Thy strong hand
and I will go on battling against the waves.
To be sure, Thou hast dragged many a man
out of the deep mud and on to the land.

If I have once extricated myself
completely from the mud,
my yearning for Thy image
will at last be real.
Then I can love strongly and wholesomely,
devoid of all shame and subterfuge,
from the very depths of my heart
and my whole soul.

On the Twentieth Sunday after Whitsun

This next poem is similarly a powerful and significant statement of
her desire for faith and her struggle to achieve it. It emanates from
the puzzling episode when Jesus speaks to the man sick with palsy
and tells him 'Be of good cheer; thy sins be forgiven thee.' The
listening scribes express their shock, and accuse Him of blasphemy,
to which He responds: 'Wherefore think ye evil in your hearts? For
whether it is easier to say Thy sins be forgiven thee; or to say, Arise
and walk? But that ye may know that the Son of man hath power
on earth to forgive sins, (then saith he to the sick of the palsy,)
Arise, take up thy bed and go into thy house.' (*Matthew* 9, 1-8)

It is not easy to connect this Gospel account, puzzling enough in itself, with the poem which Droste-Hülshoff attaches to it, and indeed the only tangible link comes as late as the sixth of the eight strophes, with what appears to be presented as a paraphrase of Christ's words: 'Forgiving is easy, healing hard'. Yet this is embedded in a whole of great beauty and majesty, as she ponders some of the deepest questions in the cycle, clothed in language and imagery rarely if ever matched elsewhere in *Das Geistliche Jahr* but reminiscent of some of her great, late, nature poems.

A poem full of thoughts of guilt and sin, remorse and the prospect of redemption, all themes so familiar in Droste-Hülshoff, culminates in one of her most beautiful expressions of optimism and faith, in the final strophe.

When dew glints on ripe ears of corn,
the sated seeds do not swell up,
and when one places a garland on the dead man,
the stiffened pulses do not flutter;
when the light passes over ruins,
not a single column is made whole,
and yet –behold! –
light and garland and dew seem like rich gifts.

Likewise, remorse can never build up
what guilt has once broken,
and yet the angels of God look mercifully
on the barren place,
and a green leaf does emerge
through the greyness of the prison-bars
towards the prisoner,
and he smiles and his soul is healed.

Ah, if only all sins could grow
like mistletoe on the branch
which has no roots and allows itself

to bloom and fade at the behest of Nature!
Yet, just as one will see on the barren tree
the traces of the clinging plant,
so does she dry up your soul and your body,
like a vampire.

Who freshens up your faith,
singed by Nature's hot breath?
Who brings back the course of your thoughts
into the pathway piously set out for them?
And the ice of your human knowledge,
that frozen stream, who loosens it,
that true river which must always separate heaven and hell?

And what your body forfeited
in the yoke of nagging feelings,
that will now remain yours for this lifetime,
and reach out also to the next.
And yet you will always be held fast
as though by a hair,
whenever a fresh spirit circles like an eagle in a fresh body.

After all, the most faithful mouth of all said:
Forgiving is easy, healing hard.
That is the ancient alliance of sin which,
consuming like the Sea of Gomorrah,
kills all the fruit in its vicinity.
And yet the marrow can thrive
and the heart of the tree force its branch upwards,
towards heaven.

Ah, only accept, only be patient!
Bear the shame of your scars willingly
and whatever your guilt has perpetrated,
lament that in silence and remorse.
Above you also is in truth the roof of heaven
and the blessing of the sun,
and ah! the dew
falls also on your burning brow.

Lord, Thou wilt not let me wander on my way,
not bid me raise my hand,
but I may stand like a column,
a sign on the barren shore,
and may hope that, when the heat of the sun
has made the rotting ruins fall away,
on that day
Thy radiance will draw aloft these little specks of dust.

On the Twenty-first Sunday after Whitsun

The Gospel reading for the day is the passage in *Matthew* (22, 1-14) which tells of the king who prepared a wedding celebration for his son and sent out his servants to invite many people to it, and, when these people would not come, sent his servants out again into the highways, to gather in the requisite number of people, good and bad. However, when he came to see all his guests gathered together, he saw one who was not dressed for a wedding, and angrily he threw him out of the celebration, into the outer darkness. The passage concludes with the famous statement: 'For many are called but few are chosen', and it is this that Droste-Hülshoff uses as the focus of her thought in this poem, which treats her own often groping, sometimes tenuous, hold on her faith. Like the casually invited guest at the wedding feast, she has no proper right to a place in the kingdom of heaven, and yet, once more, her vocation as a poet, her 'poor lamp' as she puts it, gives her a claim and provides her with the hope that the place she so desires can be hers. The poem offers not just the awareness of her role as a poet, but also an insight into what that role represents to her. As a poet, she is 'eager to instruct': this is not someone remote from her fellow human beings, inhabiting an ivory tower, but one who is willing to contribute her mite for the benefit of those who share in her suffering, the lot of all humankind.

How barren and deserted is my head on many a day,
how often is my heart entombed!
I seem senseless out of enormous weakness,
and my eyes stare across the distance unknowingly.
Ah, what an image of guilty decay!
Ah, what a wretched image of dejection!
How I do feel it! Yet not at that time
when everything is misty to me, and incomprehensible.

Shall I call it recklessness? Ah, not at all!
I feel it lying on my heart like an enormous weight.
Shall I judge it like hidden defiance?
For then I must indeed myself be lying to the master.
The strength of defiance, the cheerful display of recklessness:
these things are broken by the same stroke.
No! I am like a rotten tree-trunk,
on which the leaves hang half-starved.

If sometimes the play of nerves might cast light
upon the feverish surroundings of my muffled brow,
the springs of old wounds might spurt up
and thrust singeing life at the words.
How does my hand tremble!
How does my physical strength collapse at such a moment!
And a hard fist pushes me back,
a useless sacrifice, into its own flames.

Woe is me! Is this a wedding garment
in which I join your guests?
And may I place, oh Lord, my poor lamp, eager to instruct,
upon Thy holy coffer?
Half-drowned, I point towards the coast,
and giddy, as though confused, point upwards.
Just so did Israel wander for forty years
and searched and searched, and found a grave in the desert.

Yet Thou knowest also, my gentle Lord and Judge,
it was not vanity that guided me.
That does not light lamps for one's own decay.
He who strives still for the garlands of earthly honour

is happy to leave the lid of the coffin closed.
Yet precisely now, bereft of all Thy pounds,
I would gladly contribute a mite
for all the companions of my own suffering.

Only now have I come to know
how long it is since the waves drove me among human beings.
In my homeland - ah, my pious, lovely homeland –
loneliness must deeply sadden me.
Yet now that I have stepped into a foreign land,
how have I shuddered at companions!
They hung like mushrooms on the withered stem,
shot forth from all the plants like nettles.

Then I saw also where that could lead to,
to stand dejected on hollowed ground.
My hand could still touch the Cross,
yet I heard others rejoicing deep in the abyss.
Then I saw to whom my eyes were turning.
Then I heard what I wish to forget,
and a sound was still speaking inside me: "Oh do not stand still!
Look at those who have only stood still!"

Since then I also know to whom I have been sent:
to Him who stands there where I might not linger.
I have no light that shines or gleams,
only a voice which urges me to hurry.
Oh, hurry, hurry, only direct your footsteps!
And if no brightness breaks through the cloud,
then think : "He reigns in darkness as in light"
and in the darkness only fold your hands.

On the Twenty-second Sunday after Whitsun

The manner of Droste-Hülshoff's treatment of the story of the
healing of the nobleman's son, told briefly by St John (4, 46-53),
is very interesting, for it makes this poem stand out among the
poems of the cycle and links it somewhat surprisingly with some of

her great ballads. She supplies details not derived from the Gospel, and she creates an atmosphere which adds depth to a familiar story.

The scene is set from the beginning: the palace and the sunlight glinting on the lake, but above all the child writhing in agony, close to death, as St John makes clear, all the opulence of the royal residence contrasted with the pathetic little child in its death throes. This is a very human scene, reminiscent of the tender moments she creates in, for example, 'Der Fundator' or 'Der Tod des Erzbischof Engelberts von Köln'. The distraught mother is borne away, and the father, powerless despite his royal birth and his wealth, performs the gentle gesture of any parent watching helplessly over a dying child, wiping its brow with water, in this case brought by a slave. The poem is full of such details, and these details are of a very different kind from the analytical contemplations and juggling with thoughts so familiar from the accompanying poems.

This is indeed another example of the versatility of Droste-Hülshoff in handling her material in these mature poems, and the way in which she uses the biblical sources to extraordinary effect. The tension rises, as news comes of the approach of the famed prophet from Judæa, and all pomp and hold on power fall away, as the father makes the simple plea: 'Master, heal my son.' Anticipation gives way to disappointment as Jesus appears to reject the plea, turning away with the direction that the man should go on his way, if, as it seems, he does not believe in miracles, but the disappointment is only momentary, for the child has indeed been cured, because the father has responded to what seemed to be a rebuff with faith. Only now, for the first time in this poem, does Droste-Hülshoff connect this moving story with herself, in the simple concluding lines which speak of her own dying soul, and plead for its salvation.

The ray of sun, a golden spear,
strikes the crystal surfaces of the lake,
and, tingling about the marble sheen,
looks as though it will penetrate the walls of the palace.
The child twists and turns on silken cushions,
flailing about with its skinny little arms,
and a tear tries to force its way bitterly
out of the gentle eye
of the half-paralysed one.

Already death has laid its hand
mercilessly on its prey,
yet even if he has ice entering his heart,
it melts in his warm blood-stream.
Oh, youth, youth, how firmly
you have fettered life unto yourself,
as the creeper presses its way forward,
with roots there and threads here,
like many thousands of arms!

Oh, vision, stronger than a woman,
gnawed by waking, fear and misery!
Numbed and heavy like a dead body,
they have carried the noble lady away.
The father remains behind,
and when a slave offers refreshing water
from the stream, with cold and trembling hand
he strokes the child's soft, moist brow
and quietly whispers questions.

Who is this approaching the ear of the prince?
Menipp, the young man from Euboea.
"My lord," he utters breathlessly. "Look up.
My Lord, the prophet from Judea,
of whom the whole land speaks,
is coming, he is approaching Capernaum,
and as though bursting forth from a hundred veins,
a flood of fire is coming towards him, after him,
all around him, from Galilee."

"So, if the old gods are dead,
we must defend the new ones.
Let it be, let it be, and may my anguish
be revealed to all the people."
The horses stamp their feet. Just once
the father looks upon his dying son:
"And now onwards! What is that din?
What is it that blows against the mountain like a wind?
"My lord, the crowds of the prophet."

Oh, how fear shatters pride!
Humbly, trembling, as though preparing for some heavy task,
he does not know to whom he is speaking,
yet like the slave before the throne,
the rich man stands there, broken.
His pale lips jerk with pain,
and more feverishly than the word can express it,
much more feverishly, the fearful heart pleads: "Master, help my son!"

A murmur passes through the crowd,
cheeks flush in expectation.
"If you do not see the signs of a miracle,
then doubt must destroy you."
Thus did the Saviour speak as he turned away.
The sound of discontent was all around,
and yet a hand was raised in fear
and like a sigh there rose the soft words:
"Rabbi, my son is dying".

You have believed, and if you were as poor as Irus,
ah, whatever may torment you,
you truly wealthy man, warm with love,
you possess a treasure which no one can measure.
Oh, He who, when all was breaking,
could make it joyful and still within you,
He has heard me when I said:
Lord, my soul is dying,
oh Lord, help my soul!

On the Twenty-third Sunday after Whitsun

The parable of the debtors, as told in *Matthew* 18, 23-35 prompts this poem in which Droste-Hülshoff pours out a torrent of very personal thoughts on one of her central themes: guilt and confession of guilt, followed by forgiveness. The Gospel makes clear that forgiveness is essential for the peace of the soul. The master releases his servant from his debt, because he is moved by his plea for mercy, but the servant does not, in his turn, show the same compassion to his fellow-servant who is in debt to him. The passage culminates in the master's words and the underlining of the message: 'O thou wicked servant, I forgave thee all that debt, because thou desiredst me. Shouldest not thou also have had compassion on thy fellow servant, even as I had pity on thee? And his lord was wroth, and delivered him to the tormentors, till he should pay all that was due unto him. So likewise shall my heavenly Father do also unto you, if ye from your hearts forgive not every one his brother their trespasses.'

There is sheer agony in the self-accusation Droste-Hülshoff expresses, as she seems to search around her for a reason to forgive and finds none, and a poignant return to the theme recurrent in her youth, when she speaks of love as 'undeserved'. The mature poet, who in some of the preceding poems - though admittedly not in the one it immediately follows, with its emphasis on a raw human story - has risen to such heights of eloquence, is capable of returning to the simple pleading tone which characterises many of the early poems of the cycle. *Das Geistliche Jahr* does not present a progression, but a sometimes confusing mixture of contradictory thoughts and contrasting stylistic features.

When often, in feeble hours,
the book of my guilt opens up,
the scorpion has gnawed away
and stirred up the wounds.
Do I still know then
what I must do?
The body a mouldering yoke,
and that which is inside a ghost.

Have I then
in so short a time
committed things
which merit an eternity of shame?
I am destroyed,
I am annihilated,
and slowly my gaze
has turned away towards nothingness.

In such moments
my soul stands still,
can prompt no thought.
My will stands fettered
and I must summon up
the power of sleep
to turn the fear-filled night
to dreams.

Yet now, when my senses are clear,
my thoughts free,
my pleading can begin:
All gracious One, be with me!
At such a time,
bereft of consolation and of prayer,
oh, let thy angel
walk at my side,

that I may conquer
the dark hour in battle
and not go astray
under the spell of my fears.
Lord, Thou wilt not torment me

in vain
for Thou indeed hast a goal of rest
for souls exhausted by the chase.

If only I knew myself
how to turn the balm into poison.
Who has struck me so hard
as Thy holy scripture?
He who forgives
receives salvation and life.
How it afflicts me, Lord,
that I have nothing to forgive:

A slight unease, perhaps,
a small flame of envy:
no one has ever in my life
inflicted real pain,
and only love was undeserved.
Thus I have no sacrifice remaining
to pay the price for Thee.

Yet because Thou hast commanded it,
my mouth utters from the depth of my heart
forgiveness,
to the living as well as to the dead.
And anything else
that may come to me
in terms of hurt or shame,
whatever perhaps still on this earth

Thou hast graciously written
into the book of my future,
I cannot yearn for it enough,
value it and cherish it,
the star of hope in my agony.
Lord, be patient,
for I shall gladly repay it all.

On All Saints' Day

Droste-Hülshoff's recital of the Beatitudes from the Sermon on the Mount (*Matthew* 5,1-12) is made all the more powerful by the reiteration of the first line in the last of each strophe, and, indeed, by the relative simplicity of her language. However, the power of the poem lies surely in the final strophe with its deeply personal, beseeching tone, and the anguished cry which reverts to her familiar mode of self-accusation and her sense of alienation from other people, a note struck so forcibly in 'Not' (see pp.18-19). Interestingly that poem of as early as 1820 has one word in common with this late one: the word *Treiben* is used with similar dismissiveness in both to imply the mundane activities, the inconsequential doings, in 'Not' of other people, but here of herself. This is not the Droste-Hülshoff who prizes her poetic gift, but a woman who sees herself isolated, set apart, from others - though possibly not necessarily by her vocation - and as a result condemned to sacrifice the term 'blessed' which adheres to her fellowmen.

> Blessed are the poor in spirit,
> who at the feet of their nearest One
> are happy to warm themselves by His light
> and give Him the greeting of a servant,
> take pity on the misdeeds of a stranger,
> rejoice at the happiness of a stranger.
> Yes, at the feet of their nearest One, the poor are blessed,
>
> Blessed are the meek,
> in whom anger turns to smiling
> and the seed of gentleness sprouts no less
> from thorn and sharp spiny prickles, (f)
> whose last word is a gentle breath of love
> amidst the death rattle,

when the jerking turns to smiling.
Blessed are the meek.

Blessed are those who mourn
and eat their bread with tears,
lament only their own sin
and do not think of that of strangers,
beat their own breasts
and cast their eyes down at the guilt of strangers.
Those who eat their bread with tears,
blessed are those who mourn.

Blessed is he who is seized by thirst
for the right, for the good,
brave even on decaying ships,
bravely steering towards the waves,
should bleed to death
beneath the shore and the reefs.
For the right, for the good,
blessed those whom thirst has seized.

The merciful are blessed
who look only at the wound,
not extorting coldly and selectively,
as harm could arise,
softly and protectively,
gradually letting the balm sink in.
Those who look only at the wound, the merciful are blessed.

Ecstatically pure hearts,
the senses of spotless virgins,
to whom jesting is childish pleasure,
to whom loving is the breath of heaven,
who lit their radiant beginnings
like candles on the altar.
The senses of spotless virgins, ecstatically pure hearts!

And the pious guardians of peace are blessed,
commanding the barriers,

and the champions of unity
holding up the white banner,
gently and resolutely towards the opponent,
like the sword splitting the feather cushions.
Blessed those who command the barriers,
blessed are the guardians of peace.

Those who endure persecution for Thy sake,
Almighty Commander,
Thy hosts are blessed when they avoid everything
to preserve Thy banner for themselves.
May it never be parted from them,
neither in pleasure nor in peril.
Blessed, blessed Thy hosts who endure persecution.[1]

Thus I must call blessed all those
to whom my deeds are foreign,
must, while my wounds are burning,
remain the herald of alien happiness.
Will nothing separate me from Thee then,
wild, arid, decaying deeds?
Must I crush myself?
Will no one call me blessed?

(f). This translation is really a paraphrase: the English term is 'restharrow': 'Hauhechel' is the plant Onionis spinosa.

On All Souls' Day

This poem for All Souls' Day begins with an echo of the solemn words from St John: 'Verily, verily, I say unto you, the hour is coming, and now is, when the dead shall hear the voice of the Son of God: and they that hear shall live.' From that portentous opening, however, so familiar to the Church, comes this very intimate poem which seems to express some of the deepest thoughts of this tormented woman.

The hour is coming when the dead walk,
when long decayed eyes see.
Oh hour, hour, the greatest of all hours:
you are with me and will not let me go;
I am with you bound in duty.
I breathe for you; my wounds bleed for you.

You are terrible, and yet valuable.
Yes: my whole soul turns
towards you in life's fear and erring,
my firm refuge, my fortress,
to which unbending hope flees,
whenever fear and brooding roam like ghosts.

If I did not know that indeed
in the darkness of those places
you lay slumbering, hidden like an embryo,
then I should like to conceal my face in terror
from the light of the sun
and vanish like a pool of rain at dawn.

It is not lack of recognition that drives me towards you.
The sternest voice is gentle to me,
takes my shillings and gives millions in return.
No, where injustice has ever befallen me,
I felt at ease, and felt your soft breath
wafting through the aeons of time.

Yet love and honour urge me forward
to you as my last port,
where the inside of my grave
will appear clearly before me.
Then on the true scales my guilt and my shame
will rise up like a tower
and my fighting and my weeping will approach trembling.

I should vanish completely before you,
bereft of consolation, like a shadow.
Yet through no fault of mine
it is not like that.

My gaze stares as if motionless towards you,
as to the greatest happiness,
and I can barely, barely endure the waiting.

Yet when once hope starts,
the hand which it has placed
into the legendary depths of this bosom
will not tear from the ground like a weed
the shoot which grew up with no will of its own,
and not out of arrogance.

When the time comes,
when the vanity which the world has set out drops down,
talent and fortune, about the gaunt skeleton,
the beggar will be standing there: look at him!
Then it is time; then the lips of the poor man may,
trembling, beg for mercy.

Then a cheap and tawdry trifle will not make me blush with shame;
then the right hand will have brought me down and impoverished me,
as I deserved.
Then, from that time on, an eye full of the light of love
will not pierce me like the thrust of a dagger:
I am brought low and am redeemed.

On the Twenty-fourth Sunday after Whitsun

From the response of Christ to the Pharisees who seek to lure him
into a political trap by asking whether it is lawful to give tribute to
Caesar (*Matthew* 22,17), Droste-Hülshoff builds up a poem which
is much more generally concerned with loyalty and allegiance in
human relationships. In this respect, it is yet another departure for
her, and one which also suggests that she is nodding towards the
current political situation within the Church, with the implied
reference in the first stanza to the so-called Cologne Conflict,
which concerned the question of the baptism of infants in the case

of mixed marriages between Catholics and Protestants. It is true to say that in general her preoccupation with contemporary affairs is peripheral, but it is inconceivable that a woman of her lively intellect, especially given her family's solid Catholic faith and, in some cases, formal affiliations, would have remained altogether aloof from matters of current concern. Her reference in the first strophe reflects the then current belief that the breath of God did indeed surround the emperor or his designated substitute.

Equally, however, it is characteristic of her to express her views on more general human bonds. It is clear from her letters and the reports of conversations she had with her friends and family, and within a wider circle of associates, that people were important to her, and that she valued human contact. This was no isolated poet in an ivory tower, but a woman who could at times abandon her writing to attend to pressing family matters. That said, however, this poem leaves no doubt that her first loyalty is to God, even if the cycle as a whole raises many questions about the nature of her faith.

> Give to God that which is rightly His,
> and give it also to the emperor!
> It is His breath that hovers round the superior one.
> Do not raise your right hand, according to the sacred custom,
> not out of arrogance, not in self-will.
> But when God and the world are in conflict, my brothers,
> attach no more importance to the emperor's word than mist and smoke.
> He is the Highest One, in face of whom all power collapses,
> cracks like parched brushwood.
>
> Give to your parents, and give also to God His due.
> Oh, woe to the man who has fallen low, whose most pious inclination,
> inherent in everyone, has gone astray,
> stamping the freest man as a fortunate slave.
> Yet place the guard on the gates of awe

and keep your conscience pure and true.
He is the Father to whom you owe body and soul,
more than to any man or woman.

Love your spouse, and think in doing so of God!
He gave you His blessing when you made the vow at the altar,
firm unto the grave, placing your love and loyalty in chains,
but, if your love becomes foolishness, then keep,
oh keep, your deepest passions free!
It is to Him that you must render the tribute of a flame
which no human being shall receive.

Give your heart only to your children
in whose veins courses your own life.
Not to love the divine image
given into your hands would be bitter agony,
but if you see it hovering between happiness and guilt,
avert your eyes and hurl it down.
He, more beloved and more noble than a thousand children,
takes care of you, if your soul is heavy-laden.

And also to the friend retain that loyalty
with which is deeply bound up honour,
an earthly thing which grace has still uncovered,
as long as it does not let go the hand of virtue.
But if the hours of glittering temptation approach,
then put an end to earthly concerns
and cling to the One who at that time
can give you more than friend and (earthly) honour.

So, offer to everyone what his right demands
and take from everyone what you may receive.
Your heart may hang on delicate ribbons,
which the grace of God bestows so mercifully,
but, above that, let yearning shine forth, like a fiery star,
towards One untouched by earthly things,
towards One without whom your heart, so warm,
would nevertheless remain abandoned and wretched.

On the Twenty-fifth Sunday after Whitsun

St Matthew (9, 18-26) tells of the ruler's daughter who is lying apparently dead but whom Jesus brings back to life with the words 'the maid is not dead but sleeping'. It is this that forms the source of a poem which speaks of faith, dormant but capable of being restored to life, and it is specifically the faith of the poet herself which is referred to here as numbed, overcome with sleep, drunk even, but still able to be brought back to vitality by the Hand of God. There is a rare optimism here, a sense that the faith she so craves is truly present within her, the inheritance which can be awakened. Even here, however, the impediment is seen as reason itself, that knowledge which elsewhere is said to kill her pure faith, and which she seems so to despise. The depths of her despair are not disguised but revealed in all their cold intensity: this, as we must know, is a woman who has suffered deeply throughout her life, in search of the faith which she earnestly desires but which, ultimately one cannot help thinking, might always elude her. Yet there is solace in this poem, expressed in some of her gentlest imagery: the ray of light which falls into her dungeon, the precious stone nurtured inside her, hope bringing forth a green leaf, and faith itself folding its hands in blessing. Thus, when the poem returns in the closing strophe to the Gospel reading, it is with a confidence that her soul, like the young girl, can be healed.

> Awake, whatever is asleep! Stretch out your hand,
> Thou Saviour God. Upon my spirit lies numbness,
> a leaden band.
> It is not dead, only overcome with sleep,
> only reeling with drunkenness, a Helot, (f)
> who, in the agony of slavery, slurps noisily
> the wine which the tyrant gave to him.
> Thus that which is just lies down in me.

Yes, in the darkest hours there even so remained
for me an awareness that, still hidden as though in the cellar of my heart,
an inheritance lay sleeping, like a warm spring that trickles
down into the grave of the cavern
and leaves above the ruler's staff.
Frost, storm and snow fight for their ownership.

And the tyrant who oppresses
my best and only possession
is not idleness, nor worldly pleasure.
It is the coldly broken spirit,
ah, as I have said a thousand times,
the curse of reason which rises up defiantly
and gnaws deeply at my faith.
Alas, heavy gift, enslaved to evil powers!

At a time, black as night,
at a time which I experienced,
I was deprived of my salvation,
as the parched leaf trembles on the branch.
Bereft of consolation and devoid of hope,
unbelief was clear as the sun.
My life hung on a hair.
Oh, I would not wish such an hour (even) on bad people!

Shall I say that suffering
was increased by human travail?
I do not know what was assigned to the dust,
and yet I saw them unhappy,
laughing only to mock at cramping pain.
Boldly, yet turned to nothing, without God,
cursed yet wretched mob,
despairing of that which they would like to value.

That which did not look into the eyes of annihilation without shuddering
Was called weak.
Yet in that look lay judgment,
like the smile at the horror of death.
Why did they not leave me in peace,
Or more than that, in the cloak of friendship,

as if the physician were wielding the knife?
I do not know, but I will not argue about it.

Hear then what shielded me
from going astray completely:
that I did not employ my lack of faith
in order to raise the banner of wrongdoing,
that, even if the tree of life was felled for me,
resolve gave me the opportunity
to love the dream of my God,
and also still to wind garlands for the dead one.

Unbelief is sin, or, rather,
sin is unbelief, and it alone
can be the strongest companion
of the frosty army of all doubts.
Ah, if only I were virtuous, the darkness
would not leave me lonely.
After all, a ray of light is falling into my dungeon
because I have not allied myself completely with the bad people.

I have nurtured a precious stone for myself,
since my conscience, albeit stained,
has even so not lain in snow and ice
and has not stretched itself out in lava.
Ah, love still has breath,
hope brings forth a green leaf,
and faith, too, weary unto death,
folds its hands, as if they were offering a blessing.

Oh, Merciful One, stretch out Thy hand,
as Thou hast stretched it out to the young girl!
Tear up the bonds of muffled dreams,
so strong for me, so light for Thee!
Indeed, may Thy breath pass over,
a ray go forth from Thine eyes,
and then that which has risen again is really there,
and that which henceforth can fight in Thine army.

(f) Helot: a slave in ancient Sparta.

On the Twenty-sixth Sunday after Whitsun

There could hardly be a greater contrast with the gentle tone of the poem for the Twenty-fifth Sunday after Whitsun than this one, which immediately follows it. St Matthew's account (24,13-35) of the words of Christ predicting the Second Coming, with the echo of the words in the Book of Daniel (9,27;11,31;12,11), is the basis for this very forceful poem, from the opening question and its reference to the 'abomination of devastation'. The precise use of Luther's phrase 'Greuel der Verwüstung' forges these links with the Old and the New Testaments from the very first line, but the poem is, as so often, intensely personal, both in its content and its language and imagery. Droste-Hülshoff's originality is evident, as it is in so much of her later work, in the two striking images of the first strophe: the reference to 'the things that are close to us' sleeping 'like coal in the bed of the mine-shaft' and the scientific reference to the galvanic chain, an idea of a kind which distinguishes her markedly from her contemporaries. When she goes on to speak, in the second strophe, of what is the central theme of this poem, faith itself, it is again made more powerful because of her use of the alien image: the man of little faith 'drags his tombstone along behind him'.

Her language and the thought behind it continue relentlessly throughout this poem, which spares no-one in its impact, and one recalls her own admission, in her letter to her mother which accompanies the first part of the cycle, that she had spared no thought, not even the most secret one. Even when, in the last three strophes of the poem, she turns to herself and speaks of her own faith, or rather of the struggle to maintain it, the tone remains unyielding, and the depth of her conflict undisguised by conventional, personal terms: the reference to the 'cartilaginous heart' and the 'moksa' ensure that cool science governs the emotions she expresses, though it cannot disguise them. This is a woman, frail and suffering physically, aware, as her letters make clear, that death is not far away, but no less than ever resolute in her control and her courage to look her doubts in the face.

> Does the abomination of devastation not stand there
> in that holy place?
> Why do we dream of things that are close to us,
> as if they were sleeping like coal in the bed
> of the mine-shaft? Look up, and look about you!
> Ah, the desolation! how it struck heart on heart,
> dull and heavy, as though with a galvanic chain!
>
> Is there a place, then, that is more sacred
> than human hearts? Is there a devastation more terrible
> than when the highest thing dies of weary jests?
> Oh, faith, faith, he in whom you are cold and feeble
> drags his tombstone along behind him.
> And yet, fortunate for him if he drags it in pain.
>
> But for that man who, smiling,
> sees his jewel breaking like a child's toy,
> and as though in grace and majesty
> will pronounce a word of sympathy
> over the fool who cries for his plaything,
> yes: for him the flame went out upon the sacred hearth,
> and his nourishment exists in the swamp and in the streams.
>
> If you can bear it that the eyes see
> that towards which they turn,
> then turn your gaze in terror towards
> where the masses ferment as in the foam of decay.
> Leave that little green spot
> which only through the grace of God became the meadow of life,
> and see how they feed from your breast.
>
> Oh, if only I had never turned my feet away
> from your earth!

How do I bless you, my rich little land,
you fresh pasture of a faithful herd!
I did not see shame satisfied in you,
the lofty spirit not nestled up against all ignominy,
nor the voluptuous gesture of the deepest madness.

I am disappointed, and I have carried many a scar
out of the battle.
When devastation also beat upon my breast
and demanded the half-decayed booty,
I was torn away from it by the favour of God.
The grace is His, the guilt is mine alone.
And yet today I stand a ruin.

If I am not entirely like the desert place,
the cursed ground
where salt is strewn, pale, on stone and skull,
here and there a pillar still speaks of past splendour:
thanks be to you, my land!
You laid too early a pious band about my soul
in the hours of my childhood.

Thus I will linger and deeply oppressed
I will bear the fact
that the wall is always leaning, as though on the point of falling.
One day the battlements will still tower up anew.
There is indeed a strong and gentle hand
that out of nothingness enflames the sunburn,
and it has also borne this crumbling edifice

until today, when sighs forced their way
out of this feeble breast.
Oh, Thou who knowest even the twitching of the worm,
help me, and those, too, who are surrounded by death.
Be merciful, place on their cartilaginous heart
the moksa of suffering that it may live in pain.
Ah, Lord, they did not know what they had done!.

On the Twenty-seventh Sunday after Whitsun

No less powerful in thought but gentler in tone, as though the energy of the previous poem has given way now to a sense of relief, with passion spent, is this poem, which is based on the parable of the grain of mustard seed, small and unpretentious, which yet grows into a great tree (*Matthew* 13,31-35). There are signs here of something closer to resignation, though the suppressed struggle for faith is apparent, and there is a greater confidence that all may yet be well. The images she uses are from nature rather than from the world of science, and this is in accordance with the basic idea of growth.

Emil Staiger (p.41) calls this poem her great 'De Profundis'. The cry which resounds is less a cry of torment than one of confusion and sorrow from a soul racked by uncertainty.

> Deep, deep in many a breast sleeps a little seed.
> Yet Thou, Lord, seest it, and Thou canst bless it.
> Ah, look upon those who, unknowingly,
> do not feel the raining from Thy cloud of grace,
> those sleep-walkers vaguely banished into the life of dream
> who allow Thy dew to rise about them,
> wander about the battlements of the tower without trembling,
> not even jerking their closed eyes.
>
> I have awoken, even if to profound shame.
> Thus I shall think today not of my misery,
> but will - alas, the one thing I can do! -
> bestow a trembling prayer upon those poor creatures,
> if only a weak, half-broken breath
> which can still find the right paths
> even if it must wind its way towards Thy throne,
> as the smoky mist whirls upwards into the ether.
>
> Thou, gentle One, knowest indeed
> how to separate the warm breath of life from all earthly mist,
> Thou just One, and yet the supreme Blessing,

whose sun rises above moor and heathland,
ah, strengthen Thy ray that, sending out its glow,
it may penetrate the age-old crust.
Make the springs of stiffened blood gush forth,
and the frozen eyelid thaw.

How often in the ice-hardened ground
did I behold the little seed stretching forth!
How often from a mouth long desecrated
broke out a cry of pain which can reconcile all things.
Ah, only one who has stood in the fiery desert knows
what value to place upon the green leaf,
and only he whose ear no breath of air could soothe
can hear the half-strangulated cry.

Through my injury I have came to know
that heaven alone may weigh up sin.
Oh, may the hand of man stay at a distance,
counting life only according to the pulse-beats.
If the seed of corn does live and does not breathe,
it yet can contain a stem
which may one day splendidly unfold the branches
where the birds rejoice beneath the light.

If in ignorance the judgment of man
is hard as stone, Thou, Lord, dost know the twists and turns
of the soul and how among murderers
a sigh cries out to Thee which cannot find itself
or name itself. No fire burns so hot
as that which must worm its way through earth and stones.
No stream runs more swiftly
than that which winds its way helplessly beneath the ice.

In the curse, which all men shudder at, Thou hearest
still the cry of lamentation, devoid of strength and courage.
In the madness of the criminal there yet comes towards Thee
the beating of the shredded heart.
That is the grain of seed which as in a dream
bores its way timidly with its little roots into the earth,
and always in its mouth it bears the seed
and always within it slumbers still the tree.

Break in, oh Lord! Thou knowest the right thrust
and knowest where the wounds of sin are, faintly scarred.
Still in Thy hand lies their eternal fate,
and still lurks mutely that most terrible of hours
when Thy hand will pass to them the scales,
and damnation will rest in a man's own heart.
Oh, Jesus Christ, think of Thy agony!
Oh save those who were made from Thy blood!

On the First Sunday in Advent

The Gospel reading (*Matthew* 21,1-9) relates how Jesus rode into
Jerusalem on an ass and was greeted with cries of 'Hosanna in the
Highest!', but the background to Droste-Hülshoff's poem seems in
this case to be more complicated, possibly arising from the reading
we know she was doing at the time of the novels of Walter Scott,
but also relating to the prevailing mood of controversy within the
Catholic Church, and, finally, tinged with implied references to
the Crusades. The end-product is therefore, unsurprisingly, a
strange mixture which distinguishes it from most of the others in
the cycle, save in the overriding sense of commitment to faith.

Thou art so gentle,
so full of patience, dearest treasure, (f1)
and Thou must have such fierce champions.
Thy holy image soars above the proud banner,
and they want to bury Thy emblems
on spears and sparkling shields.

The rage of opposing forces
has armed with pride and scorn
that which bears Thy gentle name,
and already the gauntlet has been laid down,
clinking into the blood of the most holy lamb,
the sceptre upon the crown of thorns.

Thus it is true,
the rumour that is making its way through the mouth of the people,
that where Thy temple can be seen,
so gentle and so clear,
the devil builds his cell
close to the hallowed ground,
and the serpent warms itself at the altar.

When, brow against brow
and with confused cries, the champions thrust their way forward
around the sacred object
and when the brain is reeling more from the turmoil of the world,
from the exultation of victory, honour and revenge
and more tough cobwebs buzz

than should be woven, strong and pure,
into the loin-cloth of loyalty. (f2)
reddened by the beat of the heart.
Who thinks of the anguish
which pierced Thee as though with knives,
when Thou didst pray for those who crucified Thee?
Oh, Lord, are these Thy servants?

But how the curse lies upon
all those whose hand still touches the earth,
the mother of all sin.
Is it not enough that the fugitive warms himself
at the fire of the hut? Must cursed deceit
fan the fame at your hearth?

The dark spirit must avoid the man who destroyed his aspirations
for the sake of worldly possessions.
Yet, that which Thy blood, Thy sacred suffering,
achieved for us, that we should treasure on our knees
with a strong but pure spirit.

Thou Almighty One,
in these times, when it is urgent
that Thy holiness should reveal itself purely,
do not permit that blasphemy, lurking menacingly,
should cover the dregs of the yeast,
and, alas, the clear drink, too!

Allow all faithfulness
and all true and steadfast spirit
to flare up brightly and ever more brightly!
Let no sacrifice be too great
for a precious thing
and may Thy multitudes approach
ever more densely, row upon row.

But let their garments be white,
and no fold shall touch
their foreheads with gloom.
And even if the left hand
grasps the sword,
the right shall bear the olive branch.
And may their gaze be directed upwards.

Then both early and late Thou wilt,
once and today too,
recognize them as Thy champions.
Covered in perspiration and full of weariness,
humble, steadfast, prepared for peace,
thus wilt Thou name Thy multitudes,
and blessings will flow over them.

(f1) The alternative manuscript reading is 'hero' (Held) which fits in better with the surrounding imagery of battle but, in the original, loses the rhyme of 'Hort' on 'fort'

(f2) The reference is to the miraculous garment which, according to legend, protected the wearer from harm. Droste-Hülshoff may have derived the idea from a ballad by Uhland, or from Grimm (See Woesler IV, 2, p.560) or it may have been a part of popular knowledge.

On the Second Sunday in Advent

'And there shall be signs in the sun, and in the moon, and in the stars; and upon the earth, distress of nations, with perplexity; the sea and the waves roaring; men's hearts failing them for fear, and for looking after those things which are coming on the earth: for the powers of heaven shall be shaken. And then shall they see the Son of Man coming in a cloud with power and great glory. And when these things begin to come to pass, then look up, and lift up your heads; for your redemption draweth nigh.' To St Luke's report of Christ's prophesy of His coming to earth (21, 25-33), Droste-Hülshoff responds with this poem, which opens with the simple question 'Where are you, cloud, who are to bear the Son of Man?' However, the poem is not really about the Second Coming, but about the coming of faith to her, the question which taxes her most consistently in the course of *Das Geistliche Jahr*, and it is linked here with another of her favourite themes, the place of intellect in faith, and the dichotomy she feels between belief and reason. Indeed, this poem contains one of her most unambiguous rejections of reason, what she calls 'foolish reason', 'a creature made of clay', in contrast to the 'gemstone' that she cherishes within her heart, the simple faith she has craved throughout her life and which she seems at last, if only temporarily, to have achieved. The cycle as a whole leaves us knowing that the confidence she expresses here will not be lasting and that, tortured soul that she was, Droste-Hülshoff could no more lay claim to absolute confidence in her belief than she could, in the last resort, believe that the cycle was complete as she left it in 1839. Meanwhile, this gentle poem, with its constant undercurrents of questioning, is as close as we get to such confidence, although her work as a whole bears witness to the fluctuations in her thinking to the last.

> Where are you, cloud, who are to bear
> the Son of Man?
> Do I not already see the dawn rising softly
> in the east?
> The darkness lifts, time rolls gently and smoothly past.
> I see it glowing, but, ah, so pale.
>
> It is my own thoughts that well up there,
> alight,
> as though a little flame were really loosening itself

from the pond, green and covered with slime,
and swaying uncertainly in the grey mist,
surrounded by the groaning of the reeds.

Thus must the sharpest fantasy
grow weary.
Thus in the segment of the moon did I never see
the shadow of the mountain,
certain whether a colossus were taking shape,
or whether a tear were deceiving my eye.

Thus in the kingdom of the future does a figment
rise up and toss from side to side.
My thoughts without strength, pale notions.
Who will take from me the hope that I have treasured
in the depths of my heart as the precious gemstone of my poverty?

Surrender, foolish intellect!
Climb down
and light your little wick once more
on the pure fire of belief,
that wretched lamp whose faint breath
evaporates and suffocates in the fumes of its own steam.

You strange and puzzling creature made of clay,
with powers
that live and whirl about, with all your juices hissing
as though in scorn:
oh, bathe your empty feverish dream
in the one spring that has no mud and no foam.

Ward off, push away that which the Power
sends to you,
like the impertinent foe, which sends forth lightning and denies,
and turning yourself resolutely
as though towards the polar star, hold fast to that one thing,
His word, His holy word and – checkmate to the rest!

Then in the cloud you will recognize
your Lord;
then decades are not cold and far away,

and trembling you can name
the word of words, the marrowbone of life/ love (f)
if your soul remains strong in the face of the mystery.

And already today – it is in God's hands –
you can glimpse
the Saviour in the fire of the soul,
in glowing trust.
Earth and the heights of heaven may fall down,
but His words will not perish.

(f) Again, this interesting alternative in the manuscripts bears witness to her constantly evolving thought and is deliberately left here for the consideration of the reader.

On the Third Sunday in Advent

In this poem for the Third Sunday in Advent, based ostensibly on the words of Jesus in reply to the question sent by John the Baptist as to whether He is the awaited Messiah, or whether they must wait still longer (*Matthew* 11, 2-10), Droste-Hülshoff introduces the other element, alongside faith and reason: love. Of this she is more sure, as the first strophes make clear, for this love has been manifested in Christ's coming to earth, in humility, to sit as a beggar among humans. With this Saviour, God made man, who has demonstrated His love through His suffering on the Cross, she is at last able to express her unquestioning faith. It is now love that has opened up her heart, banishing thought, reason, with which she has tussled for so long in her sometimes anguished search for faith. Although the poem ends with the vision of the suffering Christ, trembling with fear in Gethsemane and bleeding on the Cross, her faith is secure in the knowledge that this is the message of love.

CHAPTER SEVEN

I am no longer waiting for anyone else.
Who is to come to me even more dear?
Who is to approach the door of my heart
so gently and yet so mystically?
Who call my name so tenderly
through the torment and the fire of fever,
a trickle of balm over and over again?

Thou hast known for all eternity
that the abundance of thoughts,
the splendour drawn from the mind
would have to shatter my brain like glass.
And so Thou camest in humility, our equal,
just as the pious ones creep up to poverty,
and sat down where the beggar sat.

When gazing all about me in confusion
has brought me to the edge of fainting,
Thou dost step forward from the hazy night,
and Thy voice whispereth softly
"Here I am, it is I, and if you will take hold of me,
then you can leave all else behind.
The prize is on my Cross!"

Oh, voice, which I have always known!
Oh word, which I have always understood!
Thou dost place upon me the rein of love
and my steps follow Thee.
In love I do believe, and wounded by love
I open up the door of my heart and the door of thought is closed.

The hunt has slowed down, chasing my footsteps
through thorns and over sharp stones.
I rest in Thy cool glade and listen to Thy gentle greeting.
The blind can see, the cold glow with warmth,
and out of the head of the madman
must emerge a host of faint shadows.

I follow Thee to the peak of mountains,
where life flows from Thy lips,

and I may see Thy tears, greeted –ah!-
a thousand times over, with salvation,
must tremble in Gethsemane,
because fear shatters the body of God,
and bloody perspiration pours over God's forehead.

Obediently He has tasted every human anguish, even unto death:
yes, unto death's vain horror,
and has drunk the full cup empty.
So, my soul creased with fear,
Pull yourself up out of the thorns and from the cavern.
Only you alone bear also an earthly house.

So let the grey ruins sway
and only mingle your tears
with the bloody dew of your Saviour,
Nature's tormented slave.
Ah, He whose sweat turned the earth red,
He knows how a sigh can be a prayer,
my Jesus, the meadow of my hope!

On the Fourth Sunday in Advent

The whole of this poem for the Fourth Sunday in Advent is placed
in the mouth of John the Baptist, according to the words of the
Gospel in response to the question from the priests and Levites:
'Who art thou?' (John 1, 19-28). The first claim is taken from the
Gospel, the famous statement of St John 'I am the voice of one who
cries in the wilderness', but the rest of the poem is Droste-Hülshoff's
own very eloquent expression of the role of John the Baptist, as the
purveyor of the Word, the representative of Christ who for the time
being remains unrecognized, though He is present in the midst of
mankind. At last there is no room for her personal doubts and
questioning here, and the result is a beautiful statement of
unambiguous confidence.

Do you ask who I am? I do not hide it from you.
I am a being without light or colour.
Do not look at me, for then your senses will turn away.
But listen, listen, listen! for I am the voice
of one who cries in the wilderness.

In nights full of pain the Word came to me
from Him who sows balm at the edge of the swamp,
who put the healing oil in the scorpion,
and for whom too the wild thorn brings forth a rose,
the dead tree-trunk ignites its spark.

So cast down your eyes and hear
from His herald the anger of your Lord,
and let His mercy, too, be known to you,
the healing of the wound as much as the black fire,
when the evil one stems the bleeding from his veins.

Take note! I know that even so within the hardest heart
a conscience slumbers unbeknown.
Take note when it awakes, and do not stifle its cry
as faithless mothers do
the whimpering of the bastard with its feeble hunch-back.

I know as well that in the whole world
altars are erected to the devil
and that many a man kneels humbly, not bowed down,
and that above the swamp like an angel
the white lotus-flower floats lightly like a little child.

The tempest of the mighty whirlpool rages
and, trembling, we flee from the monster.
The swamp lies silent, lurking like a thief.
We pick flowers and delight to see the dancing flickering
of the will-o-the- wisp.

Therefore be not warned against the despicable,
but when the aura of sweet innocence beguiles you
and the vampire smiles, step back
and sink your gaze deep, oh deep, inside you,
to see if decay is softly welling up.

Yes, wherever your eyes may turn in terror,
this day at least you are secure.
Yet often the pressure of a hand is more poisonous,
the soft tear and the silent fire,
driving the laurel away from the fury of the volcano.

I am but a breath of air: do not disdain
my feeble wafting about the One who sent me.
Wake up, wake up! You are in His kingdom,
for see: He is in your midst,
He whom you do not recognize, and I am His voice.

On Christmas Day

Not for the first time in the cycle, we have here, for the most part,
a vivid evocation, this time of the Christmas story, untroubled by
questions or ambiguities. The activity and throng outside in the
streets, the noise and confusion, all this is familiar from Droste-
Hülshoff's ballads and narratives, and when the poem then comes
to rest on the nativity scene, this is also characteristically detailed
and tender.

However, this is Droste-Hülshoff, and there are issues to be
addressed, as she does from the third strophe, which reminds us
that the context of the birth of Christ is the census decreed by
Rome, and then with the reference to the Old Testament story of
Jehu and Jezabel, the emphasis on the relationship between Israel,
subservient, and the tyrant Rome. Nor can we fail to recognize the
political implications of the birth of the Child, for He is a threat
to King Herod, and the wise men throughout the land have been
alerted to watch for His arrival, so that the scholar is anxious as he
peers out of his tent at the star. Yet, at the last, the poem returns to
the familiar nativity scene, the tiny child, the kneeling mother, and

the father, a simple man deeply perplexed and shocked at the magnitude of the events of which he is a part.

The poem lacks the personal, ravaged questioning of most of the cycle, yet it is very much a product of Droste-Hülshoff's poetic genius, brought to maturity at this late stage of her artistic development.

Through all the streets the tumult comes rolling along,
mules, camels, drivers: what sound of ringing bells,
as though the seed of Jacob were wanting once again
to move into the plain, and the sky of Judaea
lets its shining streams of sparks scatter a sapphire light
over the seething mass.

Women are walking veiled through the alley-ways,
old crones slip wearily from their loaded beast.
Everywhere shouting and pushing,
as though at the head of Jehu's chariot.
Is Jezabel once more allowing her face to rise up
out of the airy gateway of those pillars?

It is Rome, the voluptuous priestess of the gods,
the most radiant and the cruellest of the strumpets,
who is counting her slaves at this time.
With a chisel, still dripping with blood,
she engraves on tablets, heaping number upon number,
the names of the suitors whom her sword has freed.

Oh, Israel, what has become of your pride?
Have you not rubbed your hands until they bleed,
and your tears, were they seething blood?
No, when your multitudes swirl towards the market-place,
selling, bartering, haggling beneath the halls of the temple,
their courage has perished with their God.

The pillar of fire became a miserable will-o-the-wisp,
the green rod of Aaron the executioner's axe,
and the dead word lies hideously petrified,

a mummy in the Holy Book,
in which the Pharisee searches after the curse,
thundering it out over friend and stranger.

Thus, Israel, you are ripe and ready for cutting,
just as the thistle ripens in the midst of the seeds,
and as you stand there in your fierce hatred
opposite your painted, empty lover,
the two of you are equal before the rightful throne of justice,
she wet with blood and you with spittle.

Oh, melt, heaven, melt the righteous one!
You clouds, send Him as rain, the one true Messiah,
for whom Judaea does not wait,
the holy One, the gentle and the just One,
the King of Peace among the warring knaves,
come to warm that which has frozen stiff.

The night is silent. Hidden in his tent
the scholar peers anxiously
to see when the mighty tyrant of Judah will appear.
Then he lifts the curtain, staring long at the star
which glides across the face of the firmament,
like a tear of joy that heaven weeps.

And far from that tent, above a stable,
as if it were falling on to the low roof,.
it pours its light in a thousand radiuses:
a meteor! that is what the scholar was thinking
as he turned slowly back to his book.
Ah, do you know whom that lowly roof encloses?

In a manger lies a slumbering new-born child.
The mother kneels, as though lost in a dream,
wife yet virgin.
An earnest, simple man, deeply shaken,
pulls their bed close to them. His right hand trembles
as he draws her veil close around her cloak.

And at the door stand humble people,
hardworking shepherds, yet today the first to arrive.

And in the air there is a sweet and gentle singing,
lost sounds from the song of the angels:
"Glory to the Highest One, and peace to all men
who are of good will!"

On St Stephen's Day, the Second Day of Christmas

The day after Christmas Day is traditionally dedicated to St
Stephen, whose life and death by martyrdom are briefly told in Acts
6, 8-10 and 7, 54-60, passages chosen as the Epistle for that day,
the only occasion in *Das Geistliche Jahr* when Droste-Hülshoff
selects the Epistle rather than the Gospel. Stephen, the first
Christian martyr, was one of a group of converts in Jerusalem
known as the seven Hellenists, Greek-speaking Jews, as opposed to
the Aramaic-speaking Hebrews. His martyrdom is widely depicted
and his feast day has been celebrated by the Church since the
Fourth Century.

It is not surprising, therefore, that Droste-Hülshoff devotes this
poem to him, particularly since, even in Northern Europe, his feast
day was celebrated enthusiastically, after the relative calm of the
actual Christmas days, and the poem, like the biblical account of
Stephen's death, ends with the introduction of 'a young man' at
whose feet the clothes of the dead Stephen are laid. This is Saul,
who as Paul will become the Apostle whose radiance will
illuminate the whole world. It is perhaps that thought, even more
than the actual story of Stephen, which is significant for the cycle
as a whole.

Jerusalem! Jerusalem!
How often has his cry rung out!
You played without care amongst the chaos,
beneath the horse's hooves,
and the raging of the wheels.

See, that is why your city has been laid to waste,
and you are a stray chick,
ducking your head beneath the hoards of vultures.

The holy time has passed
when He was known to your senses,
and the splendour of His miracles
moves through the land only as a legend.
The wise man nods his heavy head,
the fool wishes to deny himself it,
and only pious simplicity believes
and can bear the sacrificial gift.

Oh, if it brings only a willing deed,
a faithful struggle, before the altar,
then grace will rest upon it,
a profound miracle, eternally pure.
Yet it is so. The mighty props of the present time
have been broken,
since the lightning of His signs have been concealed
from our bleak, hard senses.

Where once the swaying bridge was illuminated
and the chasm gaped clearly,
we must now seek our pathway in the mist,
a wretched bunch of people.
The priceless reward of faith
was as it were placed upon the peaks of the glacier,
and we must clamber over the ice
and, giddy, turn ourselves around on the abyss.

That which, Lord, Thou hast sent forth again and again
has really burnt our soul,
yet it remains a written word,
the living hand invisible.
Ah, only where brooding and pride
do not gnaw at the tree-trunk since time immemorial,
did the strong wood remain fresh enough
to travel freely through millennia.

Thus, alas, it is terribly true,
that many a man
as though made for the powerful mast
has braced the white sails of faith in time of danger,
and now, a dry column, naked and heavy,
announces cracking, through the blowing of the wind
that a mighty ship is sinking
in the black sea of doubt.

Oh, Saviour, send Thy lightning
to brighten for him the pious harbour
where once the strong mast was erected
to bear the lamp of Pharos.
Yes, indeed, Thy hand brings forth mountains
where cedars join with cedars.
Do not let reason be a warning light in a storm,
nor strength appear a curse!

When Stephen with his blood
sealed the meaning of Christianity,
murderers, burning with rage,
laid the dusty clothing, damp with sweat,
at the feet of a young man
who had allied himself with them,
fiercely and without a word.
And he became Paul, Christ's hero,
whose radiance illuminates the whole world.

On the Sunday after Christmas

The references to St Luke (2, 33-40) which form the basis for this poem are to the childhood of Christ, and the wondrous things which are prophesied for Him when He is brought to the temple by His parents and greeted by Simeon with the words: 'Lord, now lettest thou thy servant depart in peace, according to thy word, for mine eyes have seen thy salvation, which thou hast prepared before the face of all people; a light to lighten the Gentiles, and the glory of thy people Israel'.

However, it is only the idea of childhood which links the reference to the content of the poem, for this is probably the most obviously autobiographical of all the poems of *Das Geistliche Jahr* and sees the poet towards the close of her life, aware of her frailty at a time when we know that she had been very ill, and contemplating death. The child Jesus, doomed to die on the Cross, reminds her of the possibility of death which she has lived with for most of her life. What troubles her still, and increasingly, is the thought of her sinful state, and the poem ends most poignantly on the hope of divine mercy, though without, one senses, the conviction that this will be her lot.

> Mature in years and in accomplishment,
> I remained a child in the eyes of God,
> a naughty child full of feeble wiles
> which serve to injure me myself.
> Experience has not enriched me,
> my head is barren, my bosom empty.
> Alas: I have stored up no fruit,
> and shall never see any more seeds either.
>
> If thus the precious time were lost
> which was devoted beyond hope
> to the Being who, as yet barely born,
> was already fighting in agony for His life,
> then woe is me, who have felt death for many years
> slowly gnawing its way into my heart:
> I am playing childish games
> as if the coffin were a mummers' play.
>
> In the head of the sickly child dawns
> the uncomprehended discomfort,
> and, more fearfully, I feel my pulse beating,

like the hammering of the deathwatch-beetle.
Then the dull groaning sound arises,
the feeble cry muffled by pain,
and, stretching out like a worm,
I reach longingly for medicine.

Yet when a fresh breeze has touched the wilting,
dying nettle,
it holds itself up like a rose or a carnation
and thinks itself adorned like royalty.
Oh, foolishness, foolishness beyond compare,
as if no sigh has stirred it!
And yet I must turn pale with grief;
a sword passed through my soul.

Who could experience so much suffering
in terms of physical pain and anguish of soul
and yet in all the long years not wish
to part from the world?
Whether as a criminal he allies himself to the wheel,
or as a fool to mockery,
be merciful, oh, eternal Grace, judge him as a fool, gentle God.

Thou hast fashioned his seething brain,
not shielded from the healthy blood
the restlessly fluttering play of the nerves.
Thou knowest how to sense his dull fear,
when he winds his way among snakes,
too powerful for him and yet hated by him.
He would like to offer a sacrifice,
if only his hand can grasp it.

Thou wilt judge that which was sin,
and I must bear my punishment;
and what was confusion wilt Thou make straight,
more mercifully than I might say.
If the head is clear, the threads looser,
what then shall be my lot, I do not know.
Then can I only stammer: Saviour,
I give myself into Thy judgment.

On the Last Day of the Year (Silvester)

The tone of this poem is not one of celebration but of contemplation, and this is in accordance with the attitude which prevailed in the homeland of Droste-Hülshoff in her time. There is suspense, but this is suspense at the passing of the old year, rather than the anticipation of the new one: she waits in silence, and she is afraid. As in the immediately preceding poem, there is the awareness of impending death, and also of sinfulness: she concerns herself with the things she has done wrong, and, possibly more, with the things she has not done at all.

Above all, the poem places the dying of the year side by side with her awareness of own impending death and her sense of waste. This is no longer the poet who cherished her gift but one who seems to believe that she has squandered it. Her little lamp is going out, even though to the last the wick is sucking up the remains of the oil and she asks if her life, too, has turned to smoke. The grave awaits her, but, at the last, - and we know that she produced several different endings for this poem and that the consensus is to favour the gentler, more optimistic one offered here – the hopefulness which has asserted itself from time to time throughout the cycle, surfaces and appears to prevail. The plea for mercy is pronounced as the chime marks the end of the year.

The reference to the 'star of love' in the penultimate strophe would seem to suggest, even at this stage of her life, or perhaps particularly then, that she is aware of a vital ingredient lacking in it. Those who seek a biographical explanation would doubtless point to her failed experiences in love in her early youth, but the explanation is surely deeper, for love as a component of faith has been a major concern throughout her life, and recurrently, and in differing forms, throughout the cycle, whether because she sought it and craved it, or because, at other times, she was overwhelmed by the awareness of the love of God and her love for Him.

There can be no surprise, given what the cycle as a whole has told us that this poem ends, not at all in eager looking forward to another year, but in sombre resignation. This is the 'melody of dying'.

The year is coming to an end;
the thread unwinds itself with a whirr.
Just one short hour remaining, the final one today,
and that which once was living time
trickles like powder into its grave.
I wait in silence.

It's dead of night.
Is there perhaps an eye still open?
In these walls, Time, your passing
shudders to a close. I am afraid,
but the last hour must be lived through
awake and solitary.

Everything that I have done or thought
must be seen,
everything that arose from my head and my heart.
That stands now like an earnest guard
at the gate of heaven. Oh, half a victory,
oh, sombre fate!

How the wind tears
at the window frame!
Yes, the year is going to crumble against the shutters,
not breathe itself out like a shadow
beneath the clear and starry sky.
You child of sin!

Was not every day a hollow,
secret murmur left behind
in your barren breast,
where slowly stone broke upon stone,

when it pushed the cold breath
from the icy pole?

My little lamp is going out,
and eagerly the wick
sucks the last drop of oil.
Has my life also turned to smoke like that?
Is the hollow of the grave opening up to me,
black and silent?

Indeed my life is breaking in that circle
which the course of this year describes.
I have long known that.
And yet this heart has glowed
with the pressure of vain passions.

On my forehead simmers
the sweat of deepest fear,
and on my hand. What?
Is a star not dawning damply over there,
through the clouds?
Could it perhaps be the star of love,
showing its anger towards you with its bleak light,
that you are so afraid?

Hark! What a humming sound is that?
And there again? The melody of dying!
The bell moves its bronze mouth.
Oh Lord, I fall upon my knees!
Have mercy on my final hour!
The year is over!

BIBLIOGRAPHY

Editions

The translations in this volume have been based for the most part on the *Historisch-Kritische Ausgabe*, but other available editions have also been used where appropriate.

Annette von Droste-Hülshoff. Historisch-kritische Ausgabe.Werke.Briefwechsel, ed. Winfried Woesler, 14 vols. Tübingen: Niemeyer, 1978ff.

Annette von Droste-Hülshoff. Werke in einem Band, ed. Clemens Heselhaus, Munich: Hanser,1948

Annette von Droste-Hülshoff. Sämtliche Werke in zwei Bänden, ed. Bodo Plachta and Winfried Woesler, Frankfurt am Main and Leipzig: Insel Verlag, 2004

Annette von Droste-Hülshoff. Poems, ed. Margaret Atkinson, Oxford:Oxford University Press, 1964

Annette von Droste-Hülshoff. Das Geistliche Jahr, ed. Cornelius Schröder, Münster: Verlag Regensberg, 1951

Annette von Droste-Hülshoff. Briefe. Gesamtausgabe, ed. Karl Schulte Kemminghausen, 2 vols, Eugen Diederichs Verlag: Jena, 1944

Secondary Literature

Beuys, Barbara, *Blamieren mag ich mich nicht. Das Leben der Annette von Droste-Hülshoff*. Frankfurt and Leipzig: Insel Verlag, 1999

Gibbs, Marion E, 'Annette von Droste-Hülshoff: the poet of the ever-open wounds' in *Sappho in the Shadows*, ed. Anthony J. Harper and Margaret C. Ives, Bern etc: Peter Lang 2000, pp.223-262

Gödden, Walter, *Annette von Droste-Hülshoff. Leben und Werk. Eine Dichterchronik*, Bern etc: Peter Lang,1994

Gössmann, Wilhelm, *Annette von Droste-Hülshoff. Ich und Spiegelbild. Zum Verständnis der Dichterin und ihres Werks*, Düsseldorf:Droste, 1985

Gundolf, Friedrich, *Annette von Droste-Hülshoff*, in *Romantiker. Neue Folge*. Berlin: H.Keller, 1931

Guthrie, John, *Annette von Droste-Hülshoff. A German Poet between Romanticism and Realism*, Oxford etc: Berg 1989

Heselhaus, Clemens, *Annette von Droste-Hülshoff. Die Entdeckung des Seins in der Dichtung des neunzehnten Jahrhunderts*, Halle: Max Niemeyer Verlag, 1943

Heselhaus, Clemens, 'Das Geistliche Jahr der Droste', *Jahrbuch der Droste Gesellschaft 1948/50*, Münster: Regensberg, 1950, pp. 88-115

Heselhaus, Clemens, 'Am letzten Tag des Jahres', in *Die deutsche Lyrik*, ed. Benno von Wiese, Düsseldorf: Bagel, 1959, pp. 159-181

Mare, Margaret, *Annette von Droste-Hülshoff*, London: Methuen, 1965 (Contains some translations into English by Ursula Prideaux)

Schatzky, Brigitte E. 'Annette von Droste Hülshoff', *German Men of Letters. Twelve Literary Essays*, ed. Alex Natan, London: Oswald Wolff, 1961, pp. 81-98

Schneider, Ronald, *Annette von Droste-Hülshoff*, Stuttgart: Metzler, 1977

Schumacher, Meinolf, 'Annette von Droste-Hülshoff und die Tradition. Das *Geistliche Jahr* in literarhistorischer Sicht', *Dialoge mit der Droste*, ed. Ernst Ribbat, Ferdinand Schöningh: Paderborn etc. 1998, pp.113-145

Staiger, Emil, *Annette von Droste-Hülshoff*, Frauenfeld: Verlag Huber and Co., 1967 (3rd ed. 1st ed. Zürich 1933)

Werbick, Jürgen, '"Ist denn der Glaube nur dein Gotteshauch?". Theologische Anmerkungen zum Glaubensverständnis der Annette von Droste-Hülshoff im *Geistlichen Jahr*', *Dialoge mit der Droste*, ed. Ernst Ribbat, Ferdinand Schöningh: Paderborn etc, 1998, pp.95-111

ND - #0478 - 270225 - C0 - 229/152/20 - PB - 9781909020603 - Matt Lamination